THE SCOTTISH JUNIOR CUP 1946-1975

TOM PURDIE

AMBERLEY

First published 2011

Amberley Publishing
The Hill, Stroud
Gloucestershire GL5 4EP

www.amberleybooks.com

British Library Cataloguing in Publication Data.
A catalogue record for this book is available from the British Library.

ISBN 978-1-4456-0417-6

Typeset in 10pt on 12pt Sabon.
Typesetting and Origination by Amberley Publishing.
Printed in the UK.

CONTENTS

Acknowledgements	5
Foreword by Billy McNeill	6
Introduction	8
Hampden Park Cup Finals	
18 May 1946	13
7 June 1947	18
22 May 1948	21
21 May 1949	29
20 May 1950	33
19 May 1951	39
17 May 1952	42
23 May 1953	47
22 May 1954	51
14 May 1955	53
19 May 1956	58
18 May 1957	60
17 May 1958	64
16 May 1959	70
21 May 1960	75
20 May 1961	82
19 May 1962	85
18 May 1963	88
16 May 1964	91
15 May 1965	95
21 May 1966	102
20 May 1967	108
11 May 1968	112
24 May 1969	115
16 May 1970	119
15 May 1971	124
3 June 1972	129
28 April 1973	134
27 April 1974	141
26 April 1975	147
Appendix 1: The Junior Football Handbook	151
Appendix 2: Other Programmes	152
Appendix 3: Scottish Junior Cup Final Results	156

ACKNOWLEDGEMENTS

My thanks to the following for their assistance in the making of this book: Rodger Baillie, Bo'ness United, Bonnyrigg Rose, Cambuslang Rangers, Ricky Cantwell, Celtic, Stewart Davidson, Alison Dunlop, Evelyn Dunn, Fauldhouse United, Thom Hutchinson, George Jaconelli, Johnstone Burgh, Kilsyth Rangers, Charles Kirkwood, Linlithgow Rose, John Lister, Lachlan Mackie, Davey MacMillan, Jim McCauley, Campbell McCutcheon, David McGlone, Russell McKay, Billy McNeill, Irvine Meadow, Billy Miller, Ken Morris, Banks o' Dee, Jimmy Robertson, David Roy, Peter Rundo, St Andrews United, the Scottish Football Association, the Scottish Junior Football Association, Shotts Bon Accord, Les Smith, Robert Sneddon, Stoneyburn Juniors, Ian Strickland, Scott Struthers, Auchinleck Talbot, Bill Taylor, Gordon Watson, William Young.

FOREWORD BY BILLY MCNEILL

(Captain of the Lisbon Lions, Former Celtic Manager, and Scotland International)

I spent less than a season as a player in junior football, yet it is a part of my career that I look back on fondly and I'm delighted to write the foreword to a book that illuminates a vital part of the game in Scotland, a part that perhaps has not had the historical attention it richly deserves.

It was in the 1957/58 season that I received my baptism into junior football, with Blantyre Victoria. I had just signed provisional forms with Celtic straight from Our Lady's High School in Motherwell. The club rightly felt the step-up from schools football to senior level was too big a gap for a seventeen-year-old to straddle successfully, so I joined the Vics.

The reason for that is summed up in two words: Jock Stein. He, too, started his career with the Vics and he retained close links with their officials. Jock, at the time in charge of the Parkhead youngsters, was the man who signed me for Celtic and whatever he said about my career path was good enough for me.

The system in use then was that players from senior clubs went to junior sides for a spell. It was called farming out, and I was only one of a conveyor belt of would-be starlets who followed that route. I look back on it as the equivalent of my football National Service. I learned to take knocks, and on occasion to dish them out as well – although not always successfully. I was shown a side of football far removed from the experiences of modern-day youngsters.

Some of the facilities were far from perfect. The pitches – like so many of that era at all levels – were a long way short of the surfaces on which players ply their trade today. Yet I look back on it and don't regret a moment. It certainly toughened me up for the later part of my career.

It even prepared me to play against Rangers centre-forward Don Kichenbrand, and that was a terrifying ordeal for any youngster. I lined up against him in a reserve game, and when I was called up for an end-of-season tour in Ireland he was my opponent again, in a Bohemians Select side in Dublin. Years later I met him at a Celtic supporters' function back in his native South Africa and we had a good chat about these matches. A lovely man.

I was picked for the Irish tour because Celtic were short of four players – established first-team stars Bobby Evans, Bobby Collins and Willie Fernie were in Scotland's squad for the 1958 World Cup finals in Sweden and our skipper, Bertie Peacock, was with Northern Ireland in the tourney.

I'm convinced to this day that my spell in junior football, which lasted from September to April, helped me further my career in a beneficial way. I'll always remember the team spirit and the great lads I played alongside.

Of course, the system of grooming youngsters has changed beyond all recognition in the five decades since I was with the juniors at Blantyre Victoria, and those days are not likely to return. Now, instead of being the norm, it is almost an exception for a kid to advance from the junior ranks to senior football.

It's no use lamenting those changes; it is simply a fact of football life. Personally, I'll always remember the grounding I got in junior football, and remain to this day grateful for the experience.

INTRODUCTION

I was born in Lanarkshire and my formative years were spent in the small mining town of Shotts, whose Junior Football team was Shotts Bon Accord, formed in 1950, only four years after I had come into the world.

My mother had six brothers who were football daft, just like my grandfather, so I grew up on tales of great games and derring-do.

Inevitably, I was taken along to Hannah Park, the Bon Accord ground, to see my first ever football match. This was round about 1953 and to be honest I don't remember many details of the game other than that I began to pick weeds out of the cracks on the terracing to alleviate the boredom. When the final whistle sounded I looked around and was quite proud of my achievements; I had cleared a substantial part of the ground of weeds and had inadvertently assisted the groundsman in the upkeep of Hannah Park. But my horticultural interest soon passed and so I began my acquaintance with football in earnest.

In those days most Junior sides didn't have a management team as such and were run by members of a committee. The numbers that made up the committee could vary from club to club and it wasn't uncommon in some instances to have more committee members than actual playing staff.

My grandfather's close friend, Wattie Robertson, had a pal on the committee of the Bon Accord and as a result Wattie was privy to discussions regarding transfers, injuries and all the other pieces of gossip associated with a football club. Wattie was a character, to say the least. He wore a bulky, dark blue overcoat which he inhabited for the entire Lanarkshire winter, and a flat cap at a rakish angle. The coat was disposed of during the summer months but at the first signs of frost Wattie would once again take up residence in the huge garment. I remember well his regular visits to my grandparents' house, where Wattie would give my grandfather all the inside information with regards to what was going on behind the scenes and I would sit by the fireside wide-eyed and open-mouthed as he imparted the news. The information was always delivered in hushed tones, as if state secrets were being revealed and enemies of the crown were lurking nearby. My grandfather would receive the information with a knowing nod of the head and a pull on the pipe that was always wedged firmly between his teeth. I felt quite honoured to be party to this scene.

The previous game would then be discussed at great length. I remember that both could be very critical of the performance of certain players; praise was dished out sparingly. After one particular Shotts game, my grandfather was expounding the merits of the then-centre-forward John Hughes: 'Aye, he had no' a bad game and could be okay,' he declared. Coming from him, this was the equivalent of Hughes being awarded the Victoria Cross. This was the same John Hughes who went on to play for Celtic on 416 occasions and gained eight caps with Scotland.

It was a great time to watch football. It was an era of massive crowds that were made up with the inevitable wags and 'Terracing Tams'. The banter between spectators was often hilarious and would have done a music hall proud – so much so that sometimes the game would become a sideshow. I realised very quickly that nearly everyone who attended a game was an expert in his own right and instructions were shouted out continually to the players from the terraces on a regular basis, the most common ones being 'get the baw up the park' and 'haw you, gie yersel' a shake'. With so much advice being given to the players, I was always bewildered as to how a game could be lost. Referees were also given advice, most of which is unprintable.

But it was also a time when both teams wanted to score goals and win games, so defensive tactics were not an option. All football fans have numerous stories about the game, especially the ones who have followed the Juniors. Many are accurate, many are inaccurate, some have bits added on. Some fans adopt different versions of the same tale over the course of time.

I remember the wee guy going up and down the terracing holding a large cardboard box and shouting out, 'Erza last ae the cheese rolls!' This was followed by, 'Erza spearamint gum!' I honestly can't remember seeing anyone purchasing these mouth-watering delights but I can certainly recall the 'cairry oots'. For the benefit of the younger generation, these were quantities of beer, cheap wine, whisky etc. that had been purchased from an off-licence and brought into the ground to be consumed during the proceedings.

Someone once said that the unfortunate thing about football is that all the experts are lost to the game as they are either cutting hair or driving taxis. There's a lot of merit in that statement.

The most coveted prize in Junior Football is the Scottish Cup, first played for in 1887 when Fairfield defeated Edinburgh Woodburn three goals to one at Argyle Park, Govan in Glasgow. Forty clubs took part in the competition and the takings for the final were £16 17*s*. By 1891 over a hundred teams took part and by 1899 that number had doubled.

Understandably, during the First World War, the number of clubs competing decreased, the lowest figure being eighty-three in the 1918/19 season. However, when the hostilities ended and normality returned, the 1919/20 season saw 270 sides enter the competition and by 1922/23 this had risen to 412. The cup was won by Musselburgh Bruntonians, who defeated Arniston Rangers 3–0.

For their part, Shotts Bon Accord have won the trophy on only one occasion to date, and that was in the 1957/58 season, eight years after their formation. Despite my mother and father and me having settled in Bathgate by this time, I still travelled to Shotts most weekends and stayed at my grandparents', enabling me to watch the Bon Accord in action. I had attended all their earlier Scottish Cup games, but it was only after a 4–2 victory over Clydebank Juniors in the replayed quarter-final tie at Kilbowie Park that I realised that Shotts were only two games away from winning the prestigious trophy.

The semi-final draw presented Shotts with the enormous task of defeating Ayrshire cracks Irvine Meadow in order to reach the final. They were by far the top side of their region at that time and quite frankly no one outside of Shotts gave the Bon Accord much chance of victory. In fact, we had about as much chance as Custer's bugler had at the Little Bighorn.

The game took place in glorious sunshine at Partick Thistle's Firhill Park on 3 May 1958 in front of a crowd of 25,000. After going behind, Shotts scored twice in the second half to win 2–1. It was a fortuitous win in a great game of football. Irvine Meadow bombarded the Shotts goal for the first fifteen minutes and Boag, the Bon Accord keeper, made three outstanding saves before our rivals scored in the eighteenth minute of the first half. Shotts were then awarded a penalty, but Pat Garvie's shot was saved by Irvine's keeper, Kelpie. It was a hard-fought second half, but with fourteen minutes remaining Shotts equalised. A replay was on the cards, I thought, but with three minutes to go an Irvine defender scored an own goal and Shotts were in the final.

One of my uncles had bought me the programme for the game and it was at that game that I began to take an interest in Junior Cup programmes. The programme cost sixpence and consisted of six pages on A5, mostly advertisements. There was a photograph of the captains of the respective sides on the front cover, along with the names of the match officials. Boy, what a treasure it was for me.

The final took place on 17 May 1958, at Hampden Park, where Shotts met the less fancied Pumpherston Juniors from West Lothian. Reaching the final was a great achievement in itself; Pumpherston had only been formed in 1954 and at the outset of the competition had been 500–1 to win it.

It was my first ever visit to this famous ground and I had been briefed by my grandfather with regards to the infamous Hampden Swirl. At its worst, the spiteful wind rushed down the park to the east end of the ground, making ball control difficult. It could suddenly come to life in the goalmouth area without warning, making a goalkeeper look foolish when dealing with a cross ball.

Unlike two weeks previously at Firhill, Hampden was not bathed in sunshine. It was a dull day and the stadium looked stark, stern and grey. A cold wind blew across the pitch, making flowing football nigh impossible.

Jackie McCreary, the man who had trained and made preparations for the team since 1950, was in charge of the Bon Accord that day. Jackie was already the holder of a winner's medal, as he had played right-half for Fauldhouse United in their victory over Arthurlie at Hampden in 1946.

The programme for the final was much the same format, except for the words 'Days of Days' at the top of the front cover, and it certainly turned out that way for Shotts. They departed winners by two goals to nil, Black scoring both goals.

Back in Shotts after the game, the cup was paraded through the streets by the victorious players and the committee. After a stop at Hannah Park, it was off to the Miners' Welfare for a celebratory meal and drink.

In the town itself, the celebrations went on long into the night, even though the licensing hours were far more stringent back then. Most hostelries closed at 9.30 p.m. I think perhaps that the Lanarkshire constabulary may have turned a blind eye that evening, or even joined in some of the festivities themselves. Needless to say, for once, my grandfather and Wattie Robertson were of the opinion that their team did not have a failure in their ranks that day. I might hasten to add that this joint statement was issued at about 11 p.m. that evening after copious amounts of drink had been consumed.

Shotts Bon Accord's hold on the trophy didn't last too long, as Irvine Meadow came to town the following season in the second round and exacted revenge in the cruellest way possible by defeating the holders 4–1. Apart from the crushing defeat and the disappointment of it all, two things remain uppermost in my memory about that game. The first was that the rain that fell throughout the match was so relentless I doubted if even the famous Hollywood actor Gene Kelly would have ventured out in it. To say I was soaked to the skin would be an understatement. The second was that Scottish television cameras were at Hannah Park that day filming the game, which was shown on Scotsport later that evening and introduced by none other than Arthur Montford. For the privilege of allowing STV to film the game, the Bon Accord received a cheque for three guineas. After protesting to the Scottish Junior Football Association about the paltry sum sent by the television company, another four pounds was despatched to Shotts several months later.

Attendances at Junior Cup finals have always been healthy, but exact figures for the very early years have been difficult to obtain. The first attendance I have managed to find is the final of 1903/04, played at Celtic Park and by 10,000 spectators. However, I have traced gate receipt figures from the outset of the competition, which makes for interesting reading.

After the first ever final, which realised the sum of £16 17*s*, gate receipts continued to rise and ten years later the drawings for the final between Strathclyde Juniors and Dunfermline Juniors was £103.

The upward trend continued and, by 1905, £262 1*s* was taken at the gates for Ashfield's defeat of Renfrew Victoria.

Despite the coming of the First World War, receipts were still good and in the first final after the war, the sum of £1,720 12*s* 10*d* was received for the two matches it had taken to settle the final between Rutherglen Glencairn and St Anthony's.

During the 1920s and 1930s, the finals usually attracted crowds of between 9,000 and 22,000, depending on who the finalists were – the attendance of 28,058 for the game between Cambuslang Rangers and Benburb is a case in point. Even during the Second World War, the games were well populated and the 1942, 1943, 1944 and 1945 finals drew 24,579, 25,000, 32,000 and 25,000 respectively.

When peace reigned once again, the great post-war boom began and the crowds came to Junior games in great numbers.

In 1951, Petershill beat Irvine Meadow 1–0 in front of 77,650 fans at Hampden Park. The following year saw just fewer than 70,000 at the final between Kilbirnie

Ladeside and Camelon Juniors. Crowds were on the wane after that, and the last of the huge figures was the 1959 final between Irvine Meadow and Shettleston, which attracted 65,211.

In 1962, 49,000 supporters attended the drawn final between Rob Roy and Renfrew, but only 19,000 watched the replay. In the late 1960s until the end of the 1970s, the numbers for the finals fluctuated between 10,000 and 20,000, but by the end of the 1980s 10,000 supporters was the norm. So the halcyon days for the majority of Junior teams were over. Many clubs have since closed down due to lack of interest, especially the ones from the smaller communities. But due to the hard work of a few unpaid volunteers, namely the committees, the struggle continues to keep some clubs afloat by way of fundraising. I must mention Stoneyburn Juniors, as I now reside in Stoneyburn and I am aware of the efforts of a certain few who work tirelessly behind the scenes to provide the village with a football team. There are countless others like them throughout the land and if it wasn't for this special breed of people many other clubs would have gone to the wall by now. Stoneyburn Juniors were formed in 1928 and took up residence at Beechwood Park, where they still play. The miners who worked at the nearby Foulshiels Colliery donated a shilling from their weekly wage to enable the club to be formed and the pitch was laid with ash from the mine. The first season in existence saw them winning the Midlothian League, but thereafter their form was erratic and in the 1930/31, 1931/32 and 1933/34 seasons they finished bottom. Remarkably, the following season they were champions and they repeated this feat in 1938/39. After reaching the semi-final of the Scottish Cup in 1950, their form deteriorated and at the end of 1952/53 season they withdrew from the league, only to rejoin in 1955/56. However, financial constraints forced the club to fold at the end of 1957/58 season. In 1983, after an absence of twenty-six years, they returned to the East Region managed by John McCreadie and coached by Derek Strickland with the committee comprising of Davy MacMillan, Tom Mark, John Denholm, Billy Turner, Jimmy King, Andy Wilkins, Alex Queen and Cathie McCormack. So there is still a healthy interest in Junior Football, especially if it's your club that reaches the cup final.

Over the years I have collected programmes for the finals from 1946 onwards, and for most semi-finals. After reading John Litster's excellent book *Famous Football Programmes*, I decided to compile this book on Scottish Cup Final programmes. As John said in his tome, 'There is no better vehicle for commemorating a famous football match than its match programme!'

My ideas regarding football are most certainly old-fashioned as I was brought up on 2–3–5 formations. In my day, full-backs, wingers, centre-forwards and half-back lines were just that. I've set up the teams in this book in the 2–3–5 style.

Tom Purdie
July 2011

HAMPDEN PARK
18 MAY 1946

Attendance: 44,326

Arthurlie 0
Fauldhouse United 2 (Hynds pen., Toner)

Arthurlie: Robertson; H. Ormond, Maxwell; McKnight, Winters, Haggerty; Sloan, Johnstone, Whyte, McGarrity, W. Ormond.
Fauldhouse United: Cunningham; Welsh, Hall; McCreary, Hynds, McCreadie; Wallace, Toner, Morton, Sproule, Torley.

Semi-finals: Arthurlie 3 Polkemmet 2 (after protest)
Fauldhouse United 5 Blantyre Celtic 2

The Road to Hampden

Fauldhouse Utd		*Arthurlie*	
Armadale Th (A)	4–2	Benburb (A)	2–0
Bo'ness Utd (A)	4–3	Parkhead (A)	3–1
Forfar East End (A)	3–0	Aberdeen Caledonian (H)	6–1
Yoker Athletic (H)	3–0	Dennistoun Waverley (H)	3–2
Blantyre Vics (H)	2–2	Ardeer Recreation (H)	0–2
Blantyre Vics (A)	1–1	*(Protested)*	2–1
Blantyre Vics (N)	1–0		

The first Junior Cup final after the Second World War was won by West Lothian's Fauldhouse United. This was their forty-third game without defeat and they remained unbeaten until 27 May 1946, when they went down 6–3 to Arniston Rangers in the semi-final of the St Michael's Cup.

In the semi-finals of the Scottish cup they had overcome Blantyre Celtic 5–2 and in the previous round it had taken three games to dispose of the other side from Blantyre, 'the Vics'. After 2–2 and 1–1 draws, the sides met at Clyde's Shawfield and in front of a crowd of 22,000 Fauldhouse triumphed 2–0. In the other semi-final Arthurlie had beaten Polkemmet 3–2 but not without controversy. Polkemmet had beaten Arthurlie 3–1 but the Barrhead team lodged a protest regarding the status of Polkemmet's Willie Redpath, who it appeared had signed for Ipswich Town some years previously and had never been re-instated as a Junior. After deliberation, the SJFA ordered that the game be replayed and on 11 May in front of 32,710 at Hampden, Arthurlie won 3–2. The unfortunate Redpath went on to sign for Motherwell, where he had a long and distinguished career with the 'Steelmen', gaining nine Scotland caps in the process.

Although the population of the village was only 4,500, Fauldhouse's average attendances were 2,000 and in the week before the final they attracted 3,200 for an evening game against Polkemmet Juniors. For the final, three special trains were booked to take the fans to Hampden along with scores of bus parties. Scenes of great jubilation greeted the cup-winning side on its return to Fauldhouse on the Saturday night; they were led through the streets by the Shotts and Dykehead pipe band. It was a double celebration for the district, as near neighbours Shotts had won the Open Pipe Band Championship earlier that day. The programme for the game is thought to be the first ever produced for a Scottish Junior Cup final. It consisted of four pages of A5 black-on-white non-gloss paper. The cost of the programme was threepence and it carried one advertisement, for Afrikander tobacco, on the inside page. Above were lists of the team line-ups and match officials. On the opposite page, under the heading 'Club Gossip', was a pen picture of both sides and a résumé of how they had reached the final. This was the sixtieth year of the competition and Secretary John Kinnear of the Scottish Junior Association was proud of the fact that it had been an unbroken run: 'Neither Kaiser Wilhelm nor Adolph Hitler caused us to interrupt the competition for even one year.' An interesting fact about Fauldhouse United was that for the game they wore a red-and-white strip borrowed from Stoneyburn Juniors because of a clash of colours with Arthurlie. Another interesting fact was that the player Arthurlie had protested against, Willie Redpath, was born and raised in Stoneyburn and his family still resided there.

Headlines from 1946: In the City Chambers in Edinburgh, MPs and members of the Scottish Council for Development and Industry met and decided to petition the government to make Prestwick a trans-oceanic airport of equal standing with London's Heathrow, in order to secure Scotland's economic future. The American liberty ship *Byron Darnton* ran aground on the Island of Sanda two miles south of the Mull of Kintyre during a violent storm. The Campbeltown lifeboat responded to the ship's distress call, but because of mountainous seas and hazardous conditions it took almost fourteen hours before the fifty-four passengers and crew were rescued.

On the radio: *Letter from America*, *Dick Barton, Special Agent*, *Woman's Hour*, *Down Your Way*.

At the cinema: *The Jolson Story*, *Great Expectations*.

SCOTTISH UNIOR CUP

FINAL

Arthurlie

.. *VERSUS* ..

Fauldhouse Un.

HAMPDEN PARK, GLASGOW

SATURDAY, 18TH MAY, 1946.

KICK OFF 3 P.M.

President—Mr. S. LAWSON, Kirkintilloch.
Vice-President—Mr. JAMES FORD, Fauldhouse United.
Secretary—Mr. J. KINNEAR, Glasgow.
Treasurer—Mr. J. McARTHUR, Clydebank.

OFFICIAL PROGRAMME, 3d.

The programme for the 1946 Scottish Junior Cup final.

The Fauldhouse United team pictured with the cup at Hampden Park, Glasgow.

Captain Willie Hynds receiving the cup from Mr C. Cunningham, Glasgow's Lord Provost.

SCOTTISH JUNIOR CUP
SEMI-FINAL

ARTHURLIE
.. VERSUS ..
POLKEMMET
JUNIORS
FIRHILL PARK, GLASGOW

SATURDAY
20TH APRIL
1946
KICK OFF 3 P.M.

President—Mr. S. LAWSON, Kirkintilloch.
Vice-President—Mr. JAMES FORD, Fauldhouse United.
Secretary—Mr. J. KINNEAR, Glasgow.
Treasurer—Mr. J. McARTHUR, Clydebank.

OFFICIAL PROGRAMME, 3d.

Right: The programme for the 1946 semi-final at Firhill.

Below: Fauldhouse pictured at Shawfield for the fifth-round replay against Blantyre Vics.

HAMPDEN PARK
7 JUNE 1947

Attendance: 56,410

Shawfield 1 (Fleck)
Bo'ness United 1 (McLean)

Shawfield: Robertson; Haldane, Connel; Whitelaw, Farrell, Dougan; Beattie, Fleck, Jack, Oswald, Clark.
Bo'ness United: Stanners; Mitchell, Keenan; Paton, Stewart, Brash; Wilson, McGowan, Dickson, Pryde, McLean.

Replay attendance: 26,521

Shawfield 2
Bo'ness United 1

Semi-finals: Shawfield 3 Irvine Meadow 2
Bo'ness United 4 Renfrew 2 (after 0–0 and 1–1 draws)

The Road to Hampden

Shawfield		*Bo'ness Utd*	
St Rochs (H)	1–1	Rosyth Rec (A)	8–1
St Rochs (A)	3–0	Dundonald (H)	1–1
Bellshill Ath (H)	3–3	Dundonald (A)	5–5
Bellshill Ath (A)	2–2	Dundonald (N)	2–0
Bellshill Ath (N)	4–2	Haddington (H)	0–0
Bye	—	Haddington (A)	4–2
Larkhall Th (H)	3–3	Largs Thistle (H)	11–2
Larkhall Th (A)	3–1	Dennistoun Wav (A)	5–2
Dundee Violet (A)	4–2	Whitburn Jun (H)	4–0
Ashfield (A)	2–0		

The first game between Renfrew and Bo'ness, played at Easter Road, was watched by only 13,000 due to inclement weather. The replay at Ibrox on Saturday 10 May was played in the evening and drew an amazing 46,000, a record for the Junior Cup semi-finals. However, that record was broken the following Saturday at Hampden, when 54,414 turned up for the second replay.

This was only Bo'ness's second year in existence but already they were attracting huge crowds wherever they played. Prior to the final Bo'ness had gone thirty-five games without defeat until, due to injuries, they were forced into five positional changes to their cup-final side. Shawfield were making only their second cup-final appearance; the previous one, against Rutherglen Glencairn in 1939, had ended in a 2–1 defeat. Shawfield's goal scorer that day was Tommy Farrell, and he was the sole survivor of the 1939 final team when he took the field against Bo'ness.

The programme front had changed, with a more attractive cover printed red and black on white non-gloss paper. No advertisements were carried in the programme, which detailed the respective teams and included a pen picture of the players taking part. The programme notes spoke highly of Shawfield's Bobby Dougan, who had provisionally signed for Hearts. As it turned out, Bobby made his debut for Hearts in August of that year and was at Tynecastle until December 1954, when he joined Kilmarnock and played for the Ayrshire men before injury forced his retirement in 1960.

Headlines from 1947: HRH Princess Elizabeth married Lieutenant Philip Mountbatten at Westminster Abbey. In Scotland, displays of flags, bonfires, concerts, street parties and dances marked the occasion.
On the radio: *Round Britain Quiz*, *Twenty Questions*, *The Critics*.
At the cinema: *Possessed*, *The Farmer's Daughter*.

The programme for the 1947 final.

Scottish Junior Football Association.
SCOTTISH JUNIOR CUP
SEMI-FINAL TIE (2nd Re-play)

BONESS UNITED 4

VERSUS

RENFREW 2

at Hampden Park, Glasgow.

Saturday, 17th MAY.
1947
KICK - OF 3 P.M.

OFFICIALS:—
President—Mr. S. Lawson (Kirkintilloch R. R.)
Vice-President - Mr. J. Ford (Fauldhouse Un.)
Hon. Treasurer—Mr. J. McArthur.
Hon. Secretary—Mr. J. Kinnear.

Official Programme, 3d.

Left: The programme for the 1947 replayed semi-final.

Below: The Bo'ness side that faced Dennistoun in the fifth round in the 1946/47 season.

HAMPDEN PARK
22 MAY 1948

Attendance: 55,602

Bo'ness United 2 (Buckley, Wilson)
Irvine Meadow 1 (Fullerton)

Bo'ness United: Graham; Mitchell, Keenan; Walls, Stewart, McKee; Wilson, Pinkerton, Buckley, Sproule, Black.
Irvine Meadow: Miller; Howat, Colvin; Cousar, J. Murray, Niven; Hannah, Fullerton, Noble, Gillan, S. Murray.

Semi-finals: Irvine Meadow 1 Bathgate Thistle 0 (after two 0–0 draws)
Bo'ness United 2 Shawfield 1 (after a 0–0 draw)

The Road to Hampden

Bo'ness Utd		*Irvine Meadow*	
Loanhead Mayflower (A)	3–0	Maybole (H)	1–1
Forth Rangers (H)	3–2	Maybole (A)	1–1
Lochore Welfare (H)	6–2	Maybole (N)	6–2
Lochee Harp (H)	4–2	Lugar Boswell Th (H)	2–0
Dundee Violet (A)	2–0	Vale of Clyde (A)	5–0
Lochgelly (A)	4–2	Arniston Rangers (A)	0–0
		Arniston Rangers (H)	3–0
		Strathclyde (H)	4–4
		Strathclyde (A)	2–1
		Lesmahagow (H)	0–0
		Lesmahagow (A)	1–0

As both sides' registered colours were blue, Bo'ness changed to claret and amber for the final, the strip being borrowed from West Lothian rivals Whitburn. Irvine Meadow chose to play in a black-and-white strip. Making the final for the second year running was a great achievement for Bo'ness. The club had only been formed three years previously and only three players remained from the team that had appeared in the 1947 final. Six days after their Hampden victory, Bo'ness played sixteen games in twenty-two days between 28 May and 19 June, including a run of six games on consecutive days. Remarkably, they won the Edinburgh and District League in the last game of the season by beating Haddington by five goals to one.

The number of pages in the match programme increased to eight but it still cost threepence. The inside cover carried the lyrics for songs selected for community singing prior to kick-off. Among the songs chosen were 'Loch Lomond', 'Ho-Ro My Nut Brown Maiden', 'Cockles and Mussels', 'Tipperary' and 'Abide with Me'. The front cover changed again, with printed blue on white non-gloss paper, and the contents were far more informative, giving a list of winners since the cup's inception and various facts and figures about the competition. There were ten advertisements in the publication, one of them on behalf of the SJFA, advertising a junior international between Scotland and Eire at Hampden on the forthcoming Monday at 3 p.m. A shilling would be charged for admission. For the first time, photographs of the respective captains were shown in the programme.

By defeating Bathgate Thistle in the other semi-final, Irvine Meadow prevented an entirely East of Scotland final. One wonders what the attendance would have been otherwise, as the three ties between these sides had attracted 32,100, 27,700 and, for the final game at Ibrox Park, 33,000.

Headlines from 1948: Police in Glasgow carried out a raid on the Alba House headquarters of the Young Scotland movement and uncovered a large quantity of explosives and detonators. Several males were arrested and detained as a result of extensive police enquiries over a period of time. The group was known to hold extreme Scottish nationalist views.
On the radio: *Any Questions*, *Mrs Dale's Diary*, *Top of the Form*, *Take It from Here*.
At the cinema: *Johnny Belinda*, *The Paleface*.

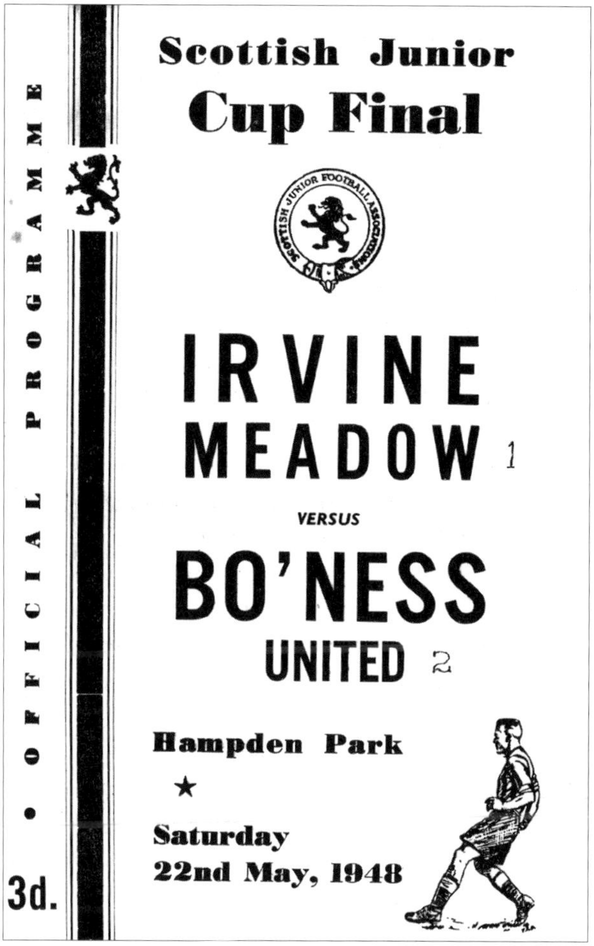

Right: The programme for the 1948 final.

Below: Alexander Walls's medal for 1948.

The reverse of the medal.

Glasgow's Lord Provost presenting the cup to captain Jamie Stewart.

Bo'ness United, Scottish Junior Cup winners 1948.

Bo'ness United's players and officials, 1948.

A souvenir booklet celebrating the cup win.

Bo'ness pictured at Easter Road for the semi-final against Shawfield, which ended 0–0.

Willie Wilson scoring the winning goal in the replayed semi-final against Shawfield Juniors.

A section of happy Bo'ness fans pictured at Hampden for the replay.

Semi-finalists Bathgate Thistle pictured at Ibrox for the game against Irvine Meadow.

HAMPDEN PARK
21 MAY 1949

Attendance: 68,837

Auchinleck Talbot 3 (McKie 2, Galloway)
Petershill 2 (Bishop)

Auchinleck Talbot: Burns; Scott, McFadzean; Finnan, Kelvin, Loneskie; McKie, Robertson, Galloway, Fraser, Goldie.
Petershill: Clark; Stewart, Ryan; J. Donaldson, Urquhart, Middlemass; McLaren, A. Donaldson, Bishop, Hughes, Armstrong.

Semi-finals: Auchinleck Talbot 2 Newtongrange Star 0 (after 1–1 draw)
Petershill 3 Benburb 1

The Road to Hampden

Auchinleck Talbot		*Petershill*	
Kllwinning Rangers (A)	2–1	Bedlay Juniors (H)	7–0
Glenafton Athletic (H)	3–0	Carluke Rovers (A)	2–0
Darvel (H)	2–1	Annbank Utd (A)	2–2
Arniston Rangers (A)	2–2	Annbank Utd (H)	1–1
Arniston Rangers (H)	2–1	Annbank Utd (N)	4–0
Dundee Stobswell (A)	2–1	Kilbirnie Ladeside (H)	3–0
Hall Russells (A)	4–1	Carnoustie Panmure (A)	2–2
Newtongrange Star (N)	1–1	Carnoustie Panmure (H)	2–2
Newtongrange Star (N)	2–0	Carnoustie Panmure (N)	3–3
		Carnoustie Panmure (N)	2–1
		Jeanfield Swifts (H)	2–0
		Benburb (N)	3–1

This final was a case of a small village club from South Ayrshire taking on the mighty Petershill, who were regarded by many as the finest Junior side in Scotland at that time. Petershill were expected to win easily and a betting man could get 3 to 1 against on Auchinleck winning the final.

The cup had not been in Ayrshire since 1924/25, when Saltcoats Victoria were winners. In those twenty-four years only one club from the Burns Country had reached the final stages, namely Irvine Meadow, who had been the beaten finalists the previous year. To reach the final, Auchinleck had taken two games to beat Arniston Rangers in the fourth round and two games to see off Newtongrange Star in the semi-final, playing a total of nine games. For their part, Petershill took an even more difficult road, playing Annbank United three times in the third round and Carnoustie Panmure on four occasions in the fifth round, so it really was unlucky thirteen for them in the final.

Once again the front cover of the programme had a different format. It was still printed on non-gloss paper and the contents remained informative, carrying pen-pictures of the players and details of the teams' progress through the previous rounds. It was interesting to note that the comments in the match programme predicting the largest ever crowd for a Junior game were spot on. Other comments were that the history of the tournament showed that the 'wee yins from the county districts' kept popping up to land a knock-out punch on their much-fancied opponents. A major advertisement in the programme were for the Scottish Farmers, informing the reader of the benefits of drinking milk and having it delivered to your door on a daily basis. The other was for the *Sporting Record*, which gave full coverage to all sports pertaining to Scotland.

Headlines from 1949: A Bengal tigress escaped from her cage at Glasgow's Calderpark Zoo after severely mauling the head keeper. The tiger was eventually shot by the director of the zoo. Fortunately, no visitors were near the cages when the animal broke free. Almost four years since the end of the Second World War, rationing was still in force, but it was announced by the President of the Board of Trade, Harold Wilson, that clothes rationing would end on 15 March.
On the radio: *Book at Bedtime*, *Morning Story*, *Ray's A Laugh*, *Billy Cotton's Bandshow*.
At the cinema: *The Third Man*, *All The King's Men*.

Right: The programme for the 1949 final.

Below: The Auchinleck players celebrating after their 3–2 win.

Above: The Auchinleck players admire the trophy in the communal bath.

Left: The programme for the 1949 semi-final at Shawfield.

HAMPDEN PARK
20 MAY 1950

Attendance: 44,402

Blantyre Victoria 3 (Gill, Swan, Rennicks)
Cumnock Juniors 0

Blantyre Vics: Warren; Gilmour, McCulloch; Allen, Young, Wright; Gill, Herbert, Swan, Lennon, Rennicks.
Cumnock: Nash; Hunter, McCartney; Knox, McCulloch, McDonald; Stewart, McLeod, Cleland, Duncan, Yuill.

Semi-finals: Blantyre Victoria 4 Stoneyburn Juniors 2 (after 0–0 and 1–1 draws)
]Cumnock Juniors 3 Ardeer Recreation 1

The Road to Hampden

Blantyre Vics		*Cumnock Juniors*	
Beith (H)	3–1	Ashfield (H)	2–1
Coltness Utd (H)	1–0	New Stevenston Utd (A)	0–0
Kilbirnie Ladeside (A)	1–0	New Stevenston Utd (H)	1–1
Carnoustie Panmure (H)	2–1	New Stevenston Utd (N)	4–2
Bo'ness Utd (H)	1–1	Dunoon Athletic (A)	2–2
Bo'ness Utd (A)	2–0	Dunoon Athletic (H)	3–1
Jeanfield Swifts (H)	2–1	Rosyth Recreation (H)	3–2
Stoneyburn Juniors (N)	1–1	Hall Russells (A)	5–2
Stoneyburn Juniors (N)	0–0	Aberdeen Parkvale (H)	5–1
Stoneyburn Juniors (N)	4–2	Ardeer Recreation (N)	3–1

The programme for this final showed a photograph of Hampden Park on the front, at the top of the page, with the Scottish Cup beneath it, printed on non-gloss white. Although the war had been over for almost five years, the programme carried a recruiting advertisement for the Territorial Army – the 5th and 6th battalions of the Highland Light Infantry. Vacancies existed for machine gunners, anti-tank gunners, 3-inch mortar crews and riflemen.

Since they were formed in 1900, this was the Vics' jubilee year. Winning the trophy made it extra-special, but oh how they made it difficult…

After wins against Coltness, Kilbirnie Ladeside and Carnoustie Panmure, it took a replay to beat Bo'ness and go on to defeat Jeanfield Swifts in the quarter finals. Then came three titanic struggles against Stoneyburn Juniors at Celtic Park before the West Lothian side were beaten 4–2. Stoneyburn's defeat in that game had been their twelfth match in the competition.

Blantyre Vics had been the first Junior club to have a game broadcast on radio, namely the Junior Cup Final of 1943/44 against Glasgow Perthshire.

This was Cumnock's first ever final in the tournament – the club had formed in 1912. They had fought hard to reach the final stages and had also been involved in replayed games en route, having had to play New Stevenson three times and Dunoon Athletic twice.

Headlines from 1950: The Stone of Destiny was stolen from Westminster Abbey and Scotland Yard issue instructions for all vehicles heading north to be searched. Scottish Nationalists were the prime suspects. Although the relic was later found and returned south, no charges were ever made. Another notable theft occurred when Blantyre's newly won trophy was stolen; it was later recovered at a disused coal mine

On the radio: *Listen With Mother*, *Twenty Questions*, *The Archers*, *Life with the Lyons*.

At the cinema: *Harvey*, *Father of the Bride*.

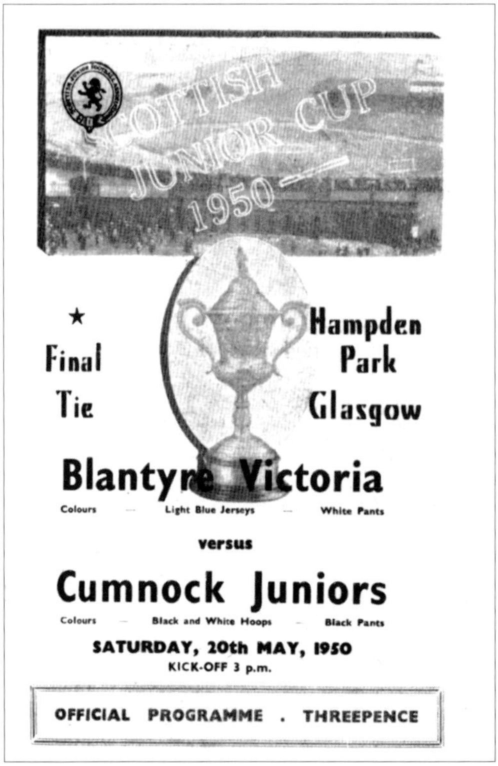

The programme for the 1950 final.

Blantyre captain Alex Young receiving the cup from Lord Inverclyde.

Blantyre's team and club officials.

Blantyre's cup-winning side.

Stoneyburn Juniors pictured at Celtic Park for the 1950 semi-final.

A newspaper cutting shows Stoneyburn coach Freddie Westbrooke addressing the West Lothian side before a Scottish cup game.

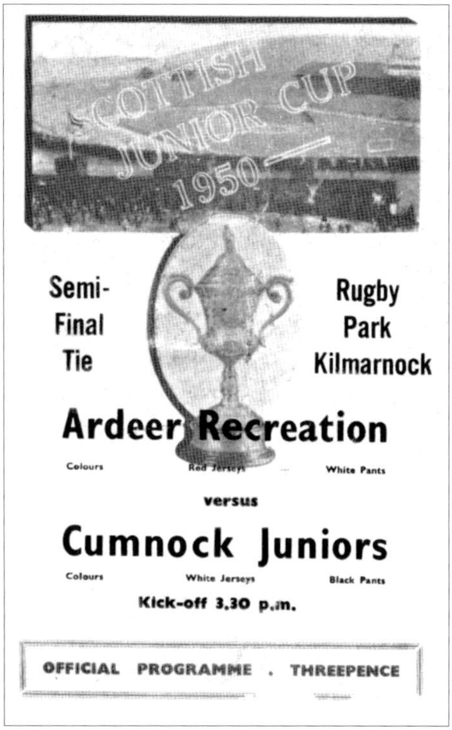

Above left: The programme for the 1950 semi-final at Celtic Park.

Above right: The programme for the 1950 semi-final at Rugby Park.

Cumnock Juniors, 1950 finalists.

Ardeer Recreation, 1950 semi-finalists.

EDINBURGH CITY F.C.

No. 1 SATURDAY, 3rd SEPTEMBER 1949

1st Round

SCOTTISH JUNIOR CUP

V.

WHITBURN F.C.

Saturday, 3rd September 1949

Nº 07

GROUND: CITY PARK, PILTON

PROGRAMME PRICE 3D.

The programme for the 1949/50 first-round tie, Edinburgh City *v.* Whitburn.

HAMPDEN PARK
19 MAY, 1951

Attendance: 77,650

Petershill 1 (White)
Irvine Meadow 0

Petershill: Stewart; McNellis, McNab; Hamilton, Shaw, Murray; Dolan, White, Bishop, McLean, Clark.
Irvine Meadow: Murdoch; Muir, Baird; Hood, McLean, Niven; Stirrat, Fullerton, McPherson, Peacock, McIntyre.

Semi-finals: Irvine Meadow 2 Broxburn Athletic 0 (after a 2–2 draw)
Petershill 3 Armadale Thistle 1

The Road to Hampden

Irvine Meadow		*Petershill*	
Coltness Utd (A)	3–0	Shawfield (H)	1–1
Pollok (A)	2–1	Shawfield (A)	2–0
Vale of Leven (H)	5–0	Glencairn (H)	0–0
Royal Albert (A)	3–1	Glencairn (A)	3–2
Blantyre Vics (A)	3–0	Cumnock (A)	0–0
Rosyth Recreation (A)	1–0	Cumnock (H)	2–1
Broxburn (N)	2–2	Camelon (H)	1–0
Broxburn (N)	2–0	Dundee Stobswell (A)	6–0
		Bo'ness Utd (H)	2–0
		Armadale Thistle (N)	3–1

This was the highest ever attendance for a Junior Cup final and remains a record to this day. Without doubt, it will never be surpassed.

Petershill's first-, second- and third-round games all required replays against Shawfield, Glencairn and Cumnock. Victories over Camelon, Dundee Stobswell, Bo'ness United and Armadale took them to the final.

By comparison Irvine Meadow required only one replay, that being the semi-final, but they were only at home once in the eight matches it took to get to the final stages. In the fifth round, they had knocked out the previous year's winners, Blantyre Vics, away from home. So the odds looked in favour of the Ayrshire team. However, it was not to be; they suffered another disappointment. The Royal Burgh of Irvine nevertheless marked the occasion with a civic reception and every player was made a freeman of the burgh.

Petershill's scorer that day, Jim White, had been called up for National Service duty with the Royal Air Force the week of the game and had to seek special leave to play in the match. I'm fairly certain that his wing commander would have been rewarded in some small way for granting a weekend pass to Airman White.

Once more, the front of the programme had been changed – this time it was printed black on white non-gloss paper, and recorded the line-ups and the match officials.

Inside were pen-pictures of the teams, head-and-shoulders photographs of both captains, and a summary of how they had progressed to the final. Advertisements were in abundance, but one in particular was for the Royal Air Force, which was seeking applicants to train to become fighter plotters and radar operators with Glasgow's Fighter Control Unit. An annual training camp was to be held each year at some RAF station in England where 'a good time is had by all'.

Headlines from 1951: In Edinburgh an estimated half-million people crowded into Princes Street to see a parade of 1,000 pipers and 500 drummers as part of the International Clan Gathering. The parade came to a halt very quickly as the sheer number of spectators prevented it going on its intended route, despite appeals by traffic and mounted police.
On the radio: *The Crazy People*, *Variety Playhouse*, *Science Review*, *Hints For Housewives*.
At the cinema: *The Lavender Hill Mob*, *The African Queen*.

SCOTTISH JUNIOR CUP

HAMPDEN PARK — FINAL TIE — SATURDAY 19th MAY

IRVINE MEADOW v. PETERSHILL

KICK-OFF 3 P.M.

Irvine Meadow (Colours: BLUE)	Petershill (Colours: MAROON)
1.—J. MURDOCH	1.—G. STEWART
2.—F. MUIR	2.—J. McNELLIS
3.—N. BAIRD	3.—R. McNAB
4.—W. HOOD	4.—A. HAMILTON
5.—J. McLEAN Captain	5.—J. SHAW Captain
6.—W. NIVEN	6.—R. MURRAY
7.—N. STIRRAT	7.—T. DOLAN
8.—T. FULLERTON	8.—J. WHITE
9.—J. McPHERSON	9.—F. BISHOP
10.—A. PEACOCK	10.—C. McLEAN
11.—J. McINTYRE	11.—R. CLARK

Referee—J. L. PROVAN, Chapelhall.
Linesmen—J. BLAIR, Arbroath and R. Gardiner, Shotts.

Official Programme Threepence

The programme for the 1951 final.

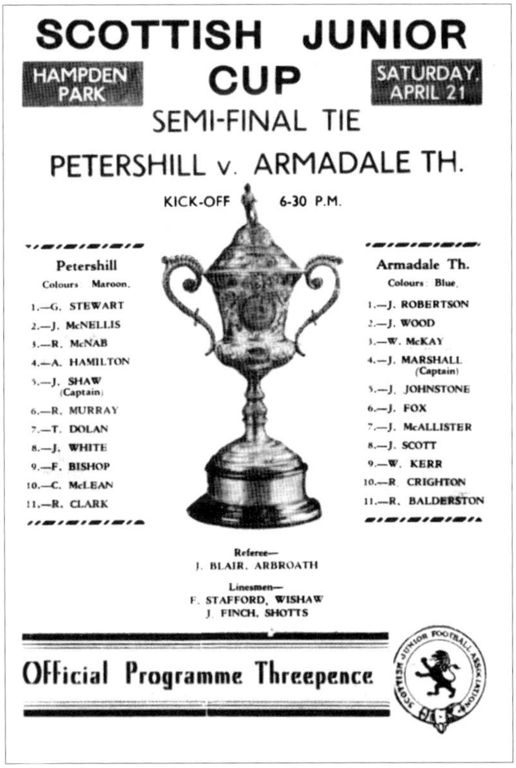
SCOTTISH JUNIOR CUP

HAMPDEN PARK — SEMI-FINAL TIE — SATURDAY, APRIL 21

PETERSHILL v. ARMADALE TH.

KICK-OFF 6-30 P.M.

Petershill (Colours: Maroon.)	Armadale Th. (Colours: Blue.)
1.—G. STEWART	1.—J. ROBERTSON
2.—J. McNELLIS	2.—J. WOOD
3.—R. McNAB	3.—W. McKAY
4.—A. HAMILTON	4.—J. MARSHALL (Captain)
5.—J. SHAW (Captain)	5.—J. JOHNSTONE
6.—R. MURRAY	6.—J. FOX
7.—T. DOLAN	7.—J. McALLISTER
8.—J. WHITE	8.—J. SCOTT
9.—F. BISHOP	9.—W. KERR
10.—C. McLEAN	10.—R. CRIGHTON
11.—R. CLARK	11.—R. BALDERSTON

Referee—
J. BLAIR, ARBROATH

Linesmen—
F. STAFFORD, WISHAW
J. FINCH, SHOTTS

Official Programme Threepence

The programme for the 1951 semi-final at Hampden.

HAMPDEN PARK
17 MAY 1952

Attendance: 69,959

Kilbirnie Ladeside 1 (Ashe)
Camelon Juniors 0

Kilbirnie Ladeside: McQueen; Ross, Ryan; Brown, Pearson, Fox; Clark, Ashe, Dunbar, E. Brown, McIntosh.
Camelon Juniors: McAllister; Ballantyne, Wilson; McKenzie, Hansen, Meiklejohn; Park, Hendry, Hamilton, Ross, Thomson.

Semi-finals: Kilbirnie Ladeside 4 Lugar Boswell 2 (after a 0–0 draw)
Camelon Juniors 2 Carnoustie Panmure 0

The Road to Hampden

Kilbirnie Ladeside		*Camelon*	
Largs Thistle (H)	3–2	Tranent (A)	2–1
Yoker Athletic (A)	2–0	Comrie Colliery (A)	5–2
Cambuslang Rangers (A)	3–2	Bo'ness Utd (A)	3–2
Auchinleck Talbot (H)	5–1	Troqueer (H)	6–0
Dalry Thistle (A)	4–0	Whitburn (H)	2–0
Annbank Utd (A)	1–0	Pollok (A)	4–2
Lugar Boswell (N)	0–0	Carnoustie Panmure (N)	2–0
Lugar Boswell (N)	4–2		

Another massive crowd was inside Hampden to watch two sides making their first ever appearance in the final of the competition. It was also Ladeside's fiftieth anniversary – their 'Jubilee Year' – and victory was the 'icing on the cake' for the Land o' Burns men. Interestingly, their goalkeeper that day was Tom McQueen, the father of Gordon, who later played for Leeds United and Manchester United and gained thirty Scotland caps. Another fascinating fact was that of the seven teams Ladeside met en route to the final, five of them were Ayrshire sides, namely Largs Thistle, Auchinleck, Dalry Thistle, Annbank United and Lugar Boswell.

Camelon Juniors were known as the Mariners because in days gone by Camelon had been a flourishing shipping port on the Forth & Clyde Canal. The club had been founded in 1921 and were the first Stirlingshire team to appear in the final since Denny Hibs played Burnbank Athletic in the 1930/31 season. The centre-half was John Hansen, father of one Alan Hansen. So on opposing sides were two players whose sons went on to play at the highest level and then become football pundits on television.

The format of the programme remained unchanged. Inside the programme, under the heading 'Wee Scottish Highlights', a schoolteacher who was allegedly well-versed in junior affairs forecast that a crowd of 100,000 would attend the final. John Kinnear, the secretary of SJFA, thought that it would be nearer 50,000. In the advertisements Eldorado Wine was on sale for 14*s* 6*d* for a full bottle and 7*s* 9*d* a half bottle.

Headlines from 1952: Television came to Scotland for the first time when the transmitter from the Kirk o' Shotts was officially opened at 7.45 p.m. on Friday 14 March. Little did we know back then how this was to change our lives and lifestyles in the years to come.
On the radio: *Sportsreel*, *The Goon Show*, *Twenty Questions*, *A Life of Bliss.*
At the cinema: *The Importance Of Being Earnest*, *Singin' in the Rain.*

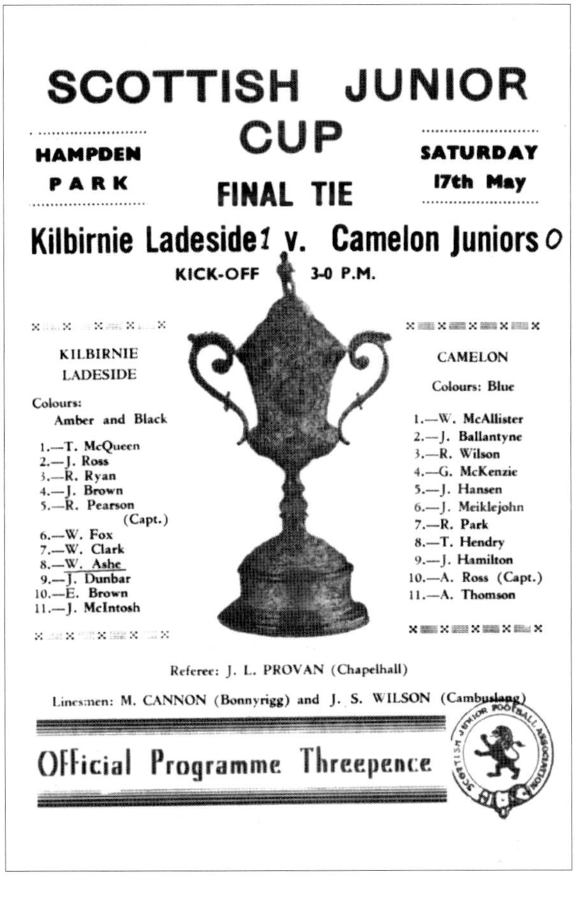
SCOTTISH JUNIOR CUP
HAMPDEN PARK
SATURDAY 17th May
FINAL TIE
Kilbirnie Ladeside 1 v. Camelon Juniors 0
KICK-OFF 3-0 P.M.

KILBIRNIE LADESIDE
Colours: Amber and Black
1.—T. McQueen
2.—J. Ross
3.—R. Ryan
4.—J. Brown
5.—R. Pearson (Capt.)
6.—W. Fox
7.—W. Clark
8.—W. Ashe
9.—J. Dunbar
10.—E. Brown
11.—J. McIntosh

CAMELON
Colours: Blue
1.—W. McAllister
2.—J. Ballantyne
3.—R. Wilson
4.—G. McKenzie
5.—J. Hansen
6.—J. Meiklejohn
7.—R. Park
8.—T. Hendry
9.—J. Hamilton
10.—A. Ross (Capt.)
11.—A. Thomson

Referee: J. L. PROVAN (Chapelhall)
Linesmen: M. CANNON (Bonnyrigg) and J. S. WILSON (Cambuslang)
Official Programme Threepence

The programme for the 1952 Junior Cup final.

Left: Kilbirnie celebrating with the trophy.

Below: An action shot shows Kilbirnie mounting an attack on the Camelon goal.

Kilbirnie Ladeside's cup-winning team.

...ing
...ws Sports Final

No. 26,276. SATURDAY, MAY 17, 1952. A KEMSLEY NEWSPAPER. 2d.

S	RESULTS POOLS		
Cope	Littl'd	V'non	Shm'n
2	–	2	2
2	2	2	–
2	2	–	2
2	2	–	2
2	2	2	X
2	2	1	2
1	2	X	2
2	2	2	1
2	2	2	2
2	X	X	2
X	2	1	2
1	2	2	2
1	2		

— Played to-morrow

Sunday's results will be found in Monday's 'News.'

24

SCOTTISH JUNIOR CUP—FINAL

Kilbirnie 1 Camelon 0

The front page of the *Evening News Sports Final* giving the result.

SCOTTISH JUNIOR CUP

RUGBY PARK

SATURDAY 12th April

SEMI-FINAL TIE

Kilbirnie Ladeside v. Lugar Boswell

KICK-OFF 3-15 P.M.

KILBIRNIE LADESIDE

Colours: Amber and Black

1.—T. McQueen
2.—J. Ross
3.—R. Ryan
4.—J. Brown
5.—R. Pearson (Capt.)
6.—W. Fox
7.—W. Clark
8.—W. Ashe
9.—J. Dunbar
10.—E. Brown
11.—J. McIntosh

LUGAR BOSWELL THISTLE

Colours: Maroon.

1.—J. Fraser (Capt.)
2.—J. Stirling
3.—D. Love
4.—J. Stewart
5.—A. Kerr
6.—J. Kelly
7.—J. Turnbull
8.—J. Skelton
9.—A. MacDougall
10.—A. Leslie
11.—J. Donnelly

Referee: J. AITKEN (Glasgow).

Linesmen: D. VIE (Paisley) and W. McALLISTER (Glasgow).

Official Programme Threepence

Scottish Junior Football Association

The programme for the 1952 semi-final at Rugby Park.

HAMPDEN PARK
23 MAY 1953

Attendance: 55,800

Vale of Leven 1 (Cassidy)
Annbank United 0

Vale of Leven: McKenzie; Gilmour, McNicol; Moran, Buchanan, Gailey; Mayberry, McKeevor, Cassidy, Moffat, Borland.
Annbank United: Neeson; Davidson, Hunter; Anderson, Livingstone, Caggie; Paton, Price, Gray, Steele, Balfour.

Semi-finals: Vale of Leven 3 Ashfield 0
Annbank United 4 Arniston Rangers 2 (after a 2–2 draw)

The Road to Hampden

Vale of Leven		*Annbank Utd*	
Maryhill Harp (A)	2–0	Dalry Thistle (H)	2–1
Lanark Utd (H)	4–2	Ardeer Recreation (A)	5–3
Baillieston (A)	2–0	Bridgeton Waverley (H)	6–3
Aberdeen Woodside (A)	4–1	Loanhead Mayflower (H)	1–1
Banks o' Dee (A)	2–2	Loanhead Mayflower (A)	2–2
Banks o' Dee (H)	6–1	Loanhead Mayflower (N)	3–1
Dunbar Utd (A)	1–1	Aberdeen Sunnybank (A)	2–2
Dunbar Utd (H)	2–0	Aberdeen Sunnybank (H)	3–0
Ashfield (N)	3–0	Crossgates Primrose (H)	2–2
		Crossgates Primrose (A)	2–2
		Crossgates Primrose (N)	3–0
		Arniston Rangers (N)	4–2

The original Vale of Leven was one of the eight clubs who, in 1873, formed the Scottish Football Association along with Queen's Park, Third Lanark, Clydesdale, Dumbreck, Eastern, Granville and Rovers. In 1926, they were playing senior football in the Scottish 3rd Division but at the end of that season the division folded. They then went on to play in the Scottish Alliance league for a few years before surrendering their senior status. Their ground, Millburn Park, lay vacant for a number of years until Vale returned to play there at Junior level in 1939.

Annbank United had also been formed in 1939 and the programme notes stated the following about them:

> Though Annbank United is only a name in the junior world since 1939, the village name goes back to the very grass roots of organised football in Scotland. Annbank were already one of the oldest clubs in the country when its name was inscribed as first winners, on the Scottish Qualifying Cup in 1895–96. However high power professionalism brought the same blight to the old Ayrshire club in time, as it did to other one time senior clubs such as Armadale, Arthurlie, Broxburn, Bathgate, Bo'ness, Beith and Vale of Leven. The curtain dropped on senior football in due course but under junior management it rose again in 1939 and it is rather an interesting coincidence that Vale of Leven should make their junior debut at the same time.

Like others before them, Annbank took the long way to Hampden by way of thirteen games. After easing past the first three rounds, they had to play Loanhead Mayflower three times before meeting Aberdeen Sunnybank. It took a replay before the Ayrshire side met Crossgates Primrose and a further three games against the Fifers before they came up against Arniston Rangers in the semi-final. This tie was also replayed and after making it to the final, defeat must have been hard to take.

The layout to the front page of the programme showed some minor changes from the previous year. The SJFA logo was now at the top and the day and date of the fixture was shown below the finalists.

Headlines from 1953: The big story was The Queen's Coronation at Westminster Abbey. In January, the Stranraer-to-Larne steamer *Princess Victoria* capsized in strong winds and heavy seas with the loss of 132 passengers and crew.
On television: *About the Home*, *Animal, Vegetable, Mineral.*
On the radio: *The Eye Witness*, *Saturday Night Theatre*, *You May Like to Hear*, *Variety Playhouse.*
At the cinema: *The Robe*, *Shane.*
Number one on 23 May: 'I Believe' by Frankie Laine.

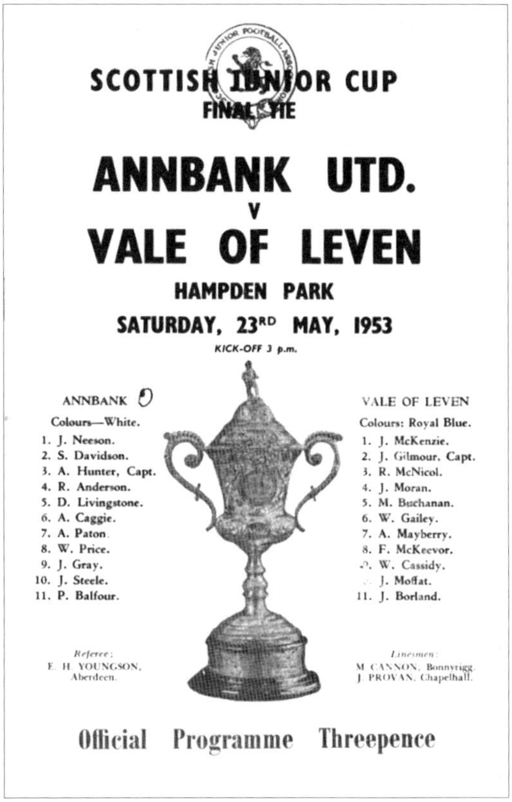

SCOTTISH JUNIOR CUP
FINAL TIE

ANNBANK UTD.
v
VALE OF LEVEN

HAMPDEN PARK
SATURDAY, 23RD MAY, 1953
KICK-OFF 3 p.m.

ANNBANK 0	VALE OF LEVEN
Colours—White.	Colours: Royal Blue.
1. J. Neeson.	1. J. McKenzie.
2. S. Davidson.	2. J. Gilmour, Capt.
3. A. Hunter, Capt.	3. R. McNicol.
4. R. Anderson.	4. J. Moran.
5. D. Livingstone.	5. M. Buchanan.
6. A. Caggie.	6. W. Gailey.
7. A. Paton.	7. A. Mayberry.
8. W. Price.	8. F. McKeevor.
9. J. Gray.	9. W. Cassidy.
10. J. Steele.	10. J. Moffat.
11. P. Balfour.	11. J. Borland.

Referee:
E. H. YOUNGSON,
Aberdeen.

Linesmen:
M. CANNON, Bonnyrigg.
J. PROVAN, Chapelhall.

Official Programme Threepence

Right: The programme for the 1953 final.

Below: Annbank mounting an attack on the Vale of Leven goal in the 1953 final.

Above left: The programme for the 1953 semi-final at Firhill.

Above right: The programme for the 1953 semi-final at Ibrox.

The programme for 1952/53 fifth-round tie, Crossgates *v.* Auchinleck.

HAMPDEN PARK
22 MAY 1954

Attendance 22,600

Aberdeen Sunnybank 2 (Chalmers, W. Stephen)
Lochee Harp 1 (Duncan)

Aberdeen Sunnybank: J. Stephen; Harper, Murray; Simpson, Scott, Garden; Chalmers, Yeoman, Cruickshank, Ingram, W. Stephen
Lochee Harp: McMahon; Jack, Pacione; Fox, Logan, McCann; Cord, Duncan, Craig, Blyth, Cochrane.

Semi-finals: Lochee Harp 2 Clydebank 0 (after a 2–2 draw)
Aberdeen Sunnybank 4 Baillieston 2

The Road to Hampden

Aberdeen Sunnybank		*Lochee Harp*	
Aberdeen Eastend (A)	2–1	Brechin Renton (H)	8–1
Woodside (A)	3–0	Johnshaven (H)	8–0
Forres Thistle (H)	7–1	Comrie (A)	5–1
Jeanfield Swifts (H)	6–0	Luncarty (H)	4–2
Petershill (H)	2–1	Musselburgh (H)	4–3
Broxburn (H)	2–1	Bathgate Thistle (A)	3–2
Baillieston (N)	4–2	Clydebank (N)	2–2
		Clydebank (N)	2–0

Previously known as Belmont FC, Aberdeen Sunnybank was formed as a juvenile club in 1936 and became a Junior side at the end of the Second World War. At that time their major problem had been securing their own ground and in the cup-winning season they were playing at Linksfield Stadium, which was a sports centre owned by Aberdeen Corporation.

They had two ambitions: to take the cup to Aberdeen for the first time and to have their own ground. Sunnybanks' first ambition was realised at 4.45 p.m. that day – and they now occupy Heathryfold Park, Aberdeen.

Lochee Harp had had their own ground since their formation in 1904, when their name was changed from Lochee Hibs to Harp. After the First World War they lost St Margaret Park to a housing development. The club shared with Dundee Violet as often as they could until 1941, when they secured a new home at Beechwood Park. Harp had always been a well-supported team and for the final they brought over 10,000 supporters to Hampden.

Headlines from 1954: Scotland took part in its first ever World Cup campaign played in Switzerland but returned home pointless after defeats by Austria 1–0 and Uruguay 7–0. By all accounts the preparations for the trip were ill-conceived and an embarrassment. The team manager was Andy Beattie, but the Scottish selection committee decreed that all team selections would be made by them. So they set off with a squad of thirteen players, two of whom were goalkeepers, leaving very little room for injuries and team changes and with no Scotland training gear, resulting in many of the players training in their club jerseys. With impeccable timing, in keeping with the shambles, Andy Beattie announced before the game against Uruguay that he was resigning from his post and stated that he had made the decision prior to leaving for Switzerland. Meanwhile Roger Bannister became the fastest miler in the world after he ran at Oxford in 3 minutes 59.4 seconds.
On television: *The Grove Family*, *Rin Tin Tin*.
On the radio: *Hancock's Half Hour*, *Hello Playmates*.
At the cinema: *Rear Window*, *The Caine Mutiny*.
Number one on 22 May: 'Secret Love' by Doris Day.

Above left: The programme for the 1954 final.

Above right: The programme for the 1954 semi-final at Pittodrie.

HAMPDEN PARK
14 MAY 1955

Attendance: 64,976

Kilsyth Rangers 0
Duntocher Hibs 0

Kilsyth Rangers: Lowe; Westwater, Mochan; O'Brien, Sievewright, Glover; Moles, Gallacher, Querrie, Forrest, Kelly.
Duntocher Hibs: Beattie; Pirie, Cleland; O'Donnell, Falconer, Scott; Callaghan, Whalen, McEwan, McDowall, Kemp.

Replay attendance: 30,000

Kilsyth Rangers 4
Duntocher Hibs 1

Semi-finals: Duntocher Hibs 4 Ashfield 0
Kilsyth Rangers 2 Armadale Thistle 0 (after a 1–1 draw)

The Road to Hampden

Duntocher Hibs		*Kilsyth Rangers*	
Larkhall Thistle (H)	5–1	Blairhall Colliery (A)	7–0
Auchinleck Talbot (A)	4–1	Crossgates Primrose (H)	6–2
Bye	—	Thornton Hibs (A)	1–1
Banks o' Dee (H)	5–4	Thornton Hibs (H)	3–2
Irvine Meadow (H)	2–1	Aberdeen Cattofield (H)	7–0
Lesmahagow (H)	5–1	Dundee Violet (A)	2–1
Ashfield (N)	4–0	Blairgowrie (A)	3–1
		Armadale Thistle (N)	1–1
		Armadale Thistle (N)	2–0

This was the first time that either of the sides had reached the final stages of the tournament. Duntocher Hibs had been formed as a juvenile club in 1894 and in

1897/98 they made the ascent to juniordom. It had been a struggle over the years to keep the club afloat and their cause was not helped when a landmine almost ruined their ground in 1943.

Kilsyth Rangers were formed in 1913 but with the outbreak of the Second World War the club had gone into temporary retirement. It was clearly the intention to restart the club when the war ended, because in 1943 a piece of land was purchased to build a new ground. The ground was named Duncansfield as it had been purchased from farmer Duncan of Ballmalloch Farm. It was made ready for Kilsyth to return to the football scene in 1945, when they joined the Central League.

In the replay, centre-forward Alex Querrie scored all of Kilsyth's goals with his head. Since he stood at 5 feet 8 inches, this was no mean feat. It was also the first time that a player had scored four goals in a final since 1928, when Gray of Maryhill Hibs had netted four in a 6–2 defeat of Burnbank Athletic. In the nine games it had taken to reach the final, Kilsyth scored an impressive tally of thirty-two goals and conceded eight.

Duntocher's scoring record was equally impressive. The team scored twenty-five goals and conceded eight in six games played. It was obviously a surprise to the 64,976 spectators when the game ended goalless. The replay made up for it, although it's interesting to note that the attendance was less than half of that of the first game.

The front cover of the programme was similar to the one used for the 1951 final. Advertising was still prominent and included R. S. McColl, His Lordship's Larder Restaurant, 4 St Enoch Place, Glasgow. The Laughing Cavalier promoted McEwan's strong ale on the back page.

Headlines from 1955: The American evangelist Billy Graham visited Scotland for the first time and more than 3,000 people were there to greet him when he arrived at St Enoch railway station, Glasgow.
On television: *Sportsview*, *What's My Line?*, *Highland Fling*.
On the radio: *Workers' Playtime*, *The Jimmy Logan Show*, *Family Favourites*, *Music to Remember*.
At the cinema: *East of Eden*, *Guys and Dolls*.
Number one on 14 May: 'Stranger in Paradise' by Tony Bennett.

SCOTTISH JUNIOR CUP

HAMPDEN PARK

SATURDAY, MAY 14th

FINAL TIE

DUNTOCHER HIBS v KILSYTH RANGERS

KICK OFF 3 p.m.

DUNTOCHER HIBS

COLOURS—
Green and White

1—R. BEATTIE
2—J. PIRRIE
3—A. CLELAND
4—P. O'DONNELL
5—J. FALCONER (Capt.)
6—R. SCOTT
7—R. CALLAGHAN
8—T. WHALEN
9—R. McEWAN
10—J. McDOWALL
11—J. KEMP

KILSYTH RANGERS

Colours: Blue

1—R. LOWE
2—W. WESTWATER (Capt.)
3—D. MOCHAN
4—J. O'BRIEN
5—W. MOLES
6—J. GLOVER
7—W. McFARLANE
8—J. GALLACHER
9—A. QUERRIE
10—M. FORREST
11—P. KELLY

Referee—
J. McLEAN, BONNYRIGG.

Linesmen—
J. L. PROVAN, CHAPELHALL.
G. STIPPIE, BELLSHILL.

Official Programme Threepence

SCOTTISH JUNIOR FOOTBALL ASSOCIATION

Right: The programme for the 1955 final.

Below: Kilsyth's Alex Querrie opens the scoring in the 1955 replay.

Lowe, Kilsyth's goalkeeper, collides with Kemp, Duntocher's forward, in the replay.

Kilsyth Rangers players and club officials.

Above: A view of Duncansfield Park, home to Kilsyth Rangers.

Right: The programme for the 1955 semi-final at Ibrox Park.

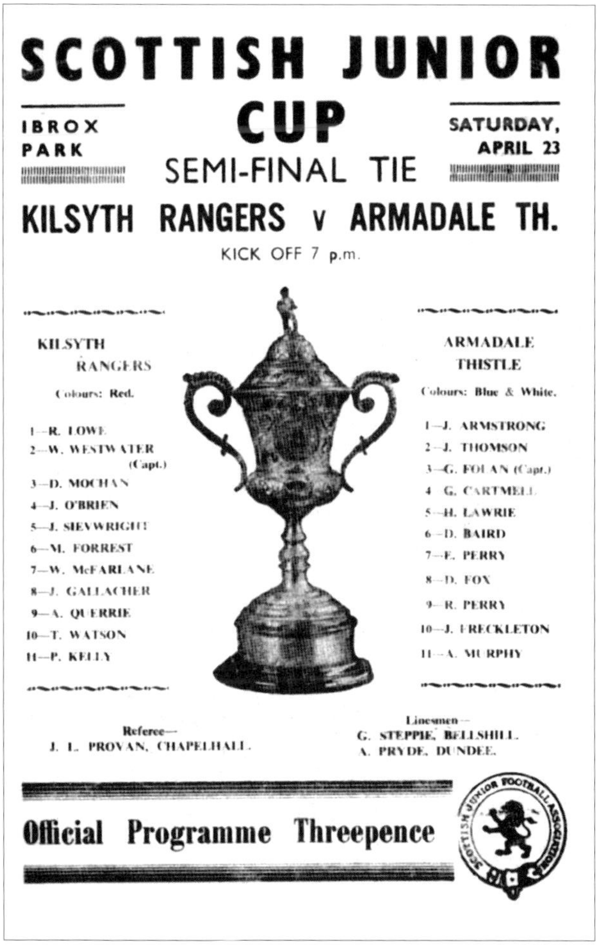

HAMPDEN PARK
19 MAY 1956

Attendance: 64,702

Petershill 4 (Stewart, Young, Hogg 2)
Lugar Boswell 1 (Sharp)

Petershill: White; McFarlane, Scobie; Turnbull, Clydesdale, Whyte; Stewart, Young, Hogg, Docherty, Burns.
Lugar Boswell: Fraser; Love, Cathie; McEwan, Baird, Donnelly; Bingham, Collins, Sharp, Neil, Wilkie.

Semi-finals: Petershill 3 Whittlets Victoria 2
Lugar Boswell 3 Broxburn Athletic 2

The Road to Hampden

Petershill	
Kello Rovers (A)	5–1
Ardrossan Winton Rovers (H)	4–1
Bye	—
Jeanfield Swifts (A)	2–2
Jeanfield Swifts(H)	4–0
Aberdeen East End (H)	2–0
Larkhall Thistle (H)	1–1
Larkhall Thistle (A)	2–0
Whitlletts Victoria (N)	3–2

Lugar Boswell Thistle	
Dreghorn (A)	0–0
Dreghorn (H)	4–2
Vale of Clyde (H)	3–3
Vale of Clyde (A)	3–0
Beith (H)	4–4
Beith (A)	3–3
Beith (N)	2–0
Alyth United (H)	5–1
Glencraig Colliery (H)	6–2
Thorniewood United (A)	2–2
Thorniewood United (H)	2–2
Thorniewood United (N)	3–1
Broxburn (N)	3–2

This was Petershill's (known as the 'Peasies') second visit to Hampden in six years; they had previously won the cup in 1951.

At that time they had two unique records in Scottish cup finals. In 1912, they recorded the highest ever win in a final when they defeated Denny Hibs 5–0, and in 1935 they were on the end of the heaviest ever defeat in the latter stages of the competition when Tranent beat them 6–1 at Ibrox Stadium.

From the Springburn area of Glasgow, the Peasies were a formidable side in the 1950s and numerous players had left to join the senior ranks. Five of the players who played in the final in 1956 – Stewart, Whyte, Hogg, Docherty and Burns – went on to join Dumbarton, Celtic, Aberdeen, Stirling Albion and Kilmarnock respectively.

Lugar, who were based 2 miles from Cumnock, were founded in 1879 as Lugar Boswell. It wasn't until they were reformed after the Second World War that 'Thistle' was added to their name. The Ayrshire side were a very good team back then and, remarkably, most of their players came from the village. The attendance of 64,702 reflected the stature of both finalists.

The front cover of the programme carried head-and-shoulders photographs of three players from each team, but the layout within was much the same. There was a full-page advertisement inside the back cover for Sellyns, a tailor's offering a wide variety of suits, raincoats, blazers, shirts and sports trousers at their branches in Glasgow. The Laughing Cavalier was still in residence on the back page, holding up a pint of foaming ale.

Headlines from 1956: Hearts beat Celtic 3–1 in the Scottish Cup before a crowd of 133,399 and took the trophy back to Edinburgh after an absence of fifty years. The Gorgie side's previous win had been in 1906, when they defeated Third Lanark 1–0 at Ibrox.
On television: *The Billy Cotton Band Show*, *Whack-O!*, *Hancock's Half Hour*.
On the radio: *At Home and Abroad*, *Have a Go*, *17 Sauchie Street*.
At the cinema: *The King and I*, *The Ten Commandments*.
Number one on 19 May: 'No Other Love' by Ronnie Hilton.

The programme for the 1956 final.

HAMPDEN PARK
18 MAY 1957

Attendance 30,800

Banks o' Dee 1 (Walker)
Kilsyth Rangers 0

Banks o' Dee: Ogston, Fowler, Robertson; Warrander, Studd, Fraser; Ewen, Walker, Anderson, McKenzie, Lornie.
Kilsyth Rangers: Lowe; McAndrew, Mochan; Robertson, Duncan, McLure; Bryans, Liddell, Querrie, McGregor, Borella.

Semi-finals: Banks o' Dee 3 Duntocher Hibs 1
Kilsyth Rangers 3 Loanhead Mayflower 0

The Road to Hampden

Banks o' Dee		*Kilsyth Rangers*	
St Clements (A)	6–0	Lochgelly Albert (A)	2–1
Locoworks (H)	6–4	Penicuick Athletic (H)	4–1
New Elgin (A)	3–1	*Bye*	—
Aberdeen East End (H)	6–3	Blantyre Vics (H)	3–0
Coltness United (H)	4–0	Glenafton Ath (A)	2–2
Newtongrange Star (H)	3– 1	Glenafton Ath (H)	3–1
Duntocher Hibs (N)	3–1	St Anthony's (H)	1–0
		Loanhead Mayfower (N)	3–0

This was Kilsyth's second appearance as finalists in two years, but only three players – Lowe, Mochan and Querrie – remained from the 1955 final team. The game was looked upon as a case of David against Goliath; Banks o' Dee from 'the Granite City' were not expected to cause a major upset against the much-fancied Kilsyth Rangers. Banks o' Dee had been formed in 1902 as the Rechabites. They had acquired the name from a strictly teetotal Rechabite group, but the story goes that several of their players at that time were fond of a pint or two, so a change of name was thought for the better. Until 1938 they were a nomadic team and played everywhere and anywhere around the city, having no place to call their own. Eventually they leased a piece at Seaton Place East. Due to the war, work was not completed until 1946, when the finished ground was unveiled and named Seaton Park. Banks o' Dee were managed by George Mutch, who had scored a last-minute extra-time goal to win the FA Cup for Preston North End against Huddersfield Town in 1938. The team prepared for the final by travelling down to Glasgow the day before the game and staying overnight in the George Hotel. After an early breakfast, they visited Hampden Park and were given a tour of the stadium before returning to the hotel for a light lunch. Prior to returning to the famous old ground, the hotel manager promised to fill the cup with champagne if they won it. What further incentive did they need?

Their preparations for the game paid off. Against all the odds, the Dee triumphed, the first and last time they have won the coveted prize.

The front cover of the programme had been completely revamped. It was printed blue and red on white glossy paper and now cost sixpence, the first increase in twenty-one years. Head-and-shoulder photographs of Alex Querrie (Kilsyth Rangers) and Dickie Ewen (Banks o' Dee) were on the front page, however the contents were still predictable, with advertisements making up most of the reading.

The programme's comments reflect on the Banks o' Dee players not receiving a signing-on fee. They had to keep their playing gear clean and had to pay their own expenses to train and play games.

Headlines from 1957: The league game at Shawfield between Clyde and Celtic attracted a crowd of almost 27,000 and Celtic won 6–3. However, the game was overshadowed by the collapse of a boundary wall, which resulted in the death of a twelve-year-old boy and many others being injured. Stricter safety measures were called for, with proper records to be kept in relation to football stadiums. However, the game would be visited by tragedy again and again and it would take many years and many other deaths and injuries before improved safety measures were put in place.

On television: *Criss Cross Quiz*, *Take your Pick*, *The Army Game*, *Murder Bag*.

On the radio: *At Home and Abroad*, *My Word!*, *Gardeners' Question Time*, *Saturday Night on the Light*.

At the cinema: *The Bridge on the River Kwai*, *Jailhouse Rock*.

Number one on 18 May: 'Cumberland Gap' by Lonnie Donnegan

Left: The programme for the 1957 final.

Below: Banks O'Dee captain Jim Warrander holds up the cup.

The programme for the 1957 semi-final at Muirton Park.

The programme for the 1957 semi-final at Celtic Park.

HAMPDEN PARK
17 MAY 1958

Attendance: 33,000

Shotts Bon Accord 2 (Black 2)
Pumpherston Juniors 0

Shotts Bon Accord: Boag; Graham, Clarke; Dundas, Hadcroft, Craig; Cruickshank, Garvie, Black, Wales, Sneddon.
Pumpherston Juniors: Bennet; Muir, Murphy; Farmer, Halpin, Johnstone; White, MacKay, Craven, Young, Berry.

Semi-finals: Shotts Bon Accord 2 Irvine Meadow 1
Pumpherston 2 Baillieston 1 (after a 2–2 draw)

The Road to Hampden

Shotts Bon Accord		*Pumpherston Juniors*	
Bridgeton Waverley (H)	0–0	West Calder United (H)	3–2
Bridgeton Waverley (A)	2–0	Dalkeith Thistle (A)	3–2
Cambuslang Rangers (H)	5–1	*Bye*	—
Bye	—	Tranent (H)	1–0
Luncarty (A)	3–1	Thornton Hibs (A)	0–0
Aberdeen Sunnybank (H)	2–0	Thornton Hibs (H)	2–1
Clydebank (H)	2–2	Parkhead (H)	3–0
Clydebank (A)	4–2	Baillieston (N)	2–2
Irvine Meadow (N)	2–1	Baillieston (N)	2–1

Again, this final was looked upon as a David and Goliath contest, with West Lothian's Pumpherston cast as David. When the competition got underway, Pumpherston were 500–1 against in the betting.

By comparison, Shotts, the crack Lanarkshire miners' team, were carrying all before them and were clear favourites to win the 'Blue Riband' of Scottish Junior Football. They were two of the youngest sides to play in a final, Shotts being formed in 1950 and Pumpherston four years later. Alas, there was to be no fairytale ending for Pumpherston. Playing right-back for Shotts that day was Tommy Graham, the older brother of George Graham, who later played for Chelsea, Arsenal, Manchester United and Portsmouth. Tommy also sampled senior football, albeit for a short time, with Dundee United.

The comments in the match programme were regarding a proposal for an all-in draw for the cup from the first round, to replace the present system whereby the first three rounds took the form of district eliminators. The proposal was due to be heard at the forthcoming annual general meeting of the SJFA.

An advertisement for Senior Service cigarettes appeared in the programme – the first appearance of tobacco in a final programme since 1946, when Afrikander tobacco was advertised.

Headlines from 1958: Peter Manuel stood trial at the High Court in Glasgow for the murder of eight people in the Lanarkshire area over a two-year period. Manuel carried out his own defence counsel, but on 29 May he was found guilty of seven of the eight charges and sentenced to death. On 11 July 1958 he was hanged at Glasgow's Barlinnie Prison and his body was buried in an unmarked grave inside the prison walls.
On television: *Val Parnell's Startime*, *Double Your Money*, *Take Your Pick*, *Wagon Train.*
On the radio: *Roundabout*, *Beyond Our Ken*, *Is there a Doctor in the House?*.
At the cinema: *Inn of the Sixth Happiness*, *Vertigo.*
Number one on 17 May: 'Who's Sorry Now' by Connie Francis.

The programme for the 1958 final.

Shotts Bon Accord's cup-winning side.

Centre-forward Black scoring the second of his two goals.

Shotts keeper John Boag celebrates the goal.

Captain Sam Hadcroft and the team arriving at Hannah Park, Shotts.

The champagne flows in the dressing room.

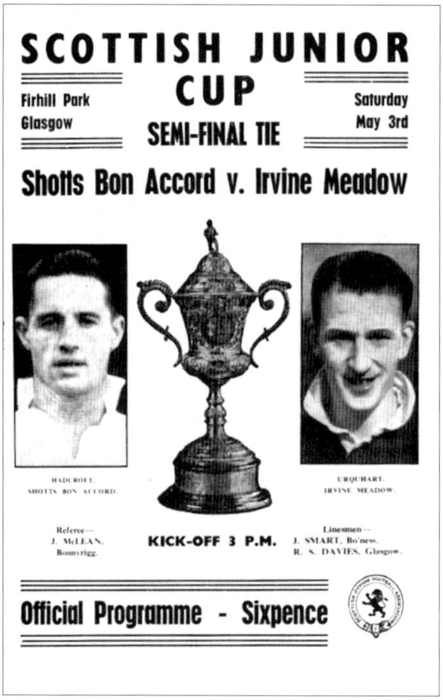

Above left: The programme for 1958 semi- final at Firhill.

Above right: The programme for the 1958 semi-final at Brockville.

Pumpherston Juniors, 1957/58 finalists.

Joe Young, Vince Halpin and Dave Johnstone of Pumpherston Juniors.

HAMPDEN PARK
16 MAY 1959

Attendance: 65,211

Irvine Meadow 2 (Morrison 2 Pens)
Shettleston Juniors 1 (Sim)

Irvine Meadow: Prentice; Hughes, Isaacs; Dickie, Crawford, Carr; Carroll, Curran, Wark, Morrison, Walker.
Shettleston Juniors: Brown; Reid, Sim; Sinclair, Bell, Duncanson; Graham, Black, O'Brien, Wright, Quinn.

Semi-Finals: Irvine Meadow 2 Carluke Rovers 1
Shettleston Juniors 1 Johnstone Burgh 0

The Road to Hampden

Shettleston		*Irvine Meadow*	
Bellshill Athletic (H)	2–0	Greenock (H)	3–2
Troon (H)	2–0	Shotts Bon Accord (A)	4–1
Larkhall Thistle (H)	3–1	*Bye*	—
Kirrie Thistle (A)	4–2	Jeanfield Swifts (A)	7–1
Lanark United (H)	2–1	Aberdeen Lads Club (A)	3–1
Easthouses Lily (H)	3–0	Blairgowrie (H)	2–2
Johnstone Burgh (N)	1–0	Blairgowrie (A)	5–1
		Carluke Rovers (N)	2–1

This was to be the last of the huge crowds at Hampden for a final. In the 1960s the crowds would fall alarmingly, sometimes dipping as low as 10,000.

Founded in 1897, Irvine Meadow were making their third appearance at Hampden, hoping to make it third time lucky, having been beaten as finalists in 1948 and 1951. They had already disposed of the previous year's winners, Shotts Bon Accord, on the way to the final, and with a very experienced team they were expected to win.

Shettleston had been formed in 1903 but this was their first ever cup final. Over the years they had made little or no impact on the tournament. Indeed, their only previous semi-final appearance had been in 1925, when Saltcoats Victoria had defeated them 2–1 at Love Street, Paisley. The club's run of bad luck was to continue.

A photograph of Shettleston's half-back line of Sinclair, Bell and Duncanson was on the front of the programme, as was one of Irvine's inside trio of Curran, Wark and Morrison.

Burns & Laird was advertising trips on the *Royal Ulsterman* and *Royal Scotsman* from Glasgow to Belfast and from Glasgow to Dublin on the inside cover.

Headlines from 1959: Forty-six men were killed at the Auchengeich Colliery, Chryston, Lanarkshire. The men were travelling to the coal face for their first shift after a three-day strike. An electrical fault was thought to have triggered the disaster, causing the men to be trapped behind a wall of flames, deep underground. It was Scotland's worst pit disaster of the century.
On television: *Concentration*, *Play of the Week*, *The Arthur Haynes Show*, *Spot the Tune*.
On the radio: *Pick of the Week*, *Housewives' Choice*, *Family Favourites*.
At the cinema: *Some Like It Hot*, *Ben Hur*.
Number one on 16 May: 'A Fool Such As I' by Elvis Presley.

The programme for the 1959 final.

Irvine Meadow in 1959.

Irvine Meadow's cup-winning side.

Above: Morrison scores Irvine Meadow's second goal from the spot.

Right: The programme for the 1959 semi-final at Firhill Park.

The Johnstone Burgh side that reached the 1959 semi-finals.

Shettleston at Celtic Park for the 1959 semi-final against Johnstone.

HAMPDEN PARK
21 MAY 1960

Attendance: 34,603

St Andrews United 3 (Borella 2, W. Penman)
Greenock Juniors 1 (McKellar)

St Andrews United: Lister; W. P. Penman, Hughes; Crookston, Davidson, Wills; Carmichael, Fraser, Smith, W. Penman, Borella.
Greenock Juniors: McGinley; Reilly, Hogg; Stewart, Buchanan, Brabender; Gibson, McCartney, McKellar, Samuel, Winter.

Semi-finals: St Andrews United 2 Thornton Hibs 1 (after a 1–1 draw)
Greenock Juniors 2 Ardeer Thistle 0 (after a 3–3 draw)

The Road to Hampden

St Andrews United		*Greenock Juniors*	
Haddington Athletic (H)	5–0	Kello Rovers (H)	3–2
Bonnybridge (H)	6–2	Lugar Boswell (H)	6–0
Bye	—	Rob Roy (A)	2–0
Drumlemble (H)	6–1	*(Protested)*	3–1
Banks o' Dee (A)	2–1	Lochee Harp (H)	2–1
Dunipace (A)	4–1	Larkhall Thistle (A)	3–1
Thornton Hibs (N)	1–1	Johnstone Burgh (H)	1–1
Thornton Hibs (N)	2–1	Johnstone Burgh (A)	3–1
		Ardeer Thistle (N)	3–3
		Ardeer Thistle (N)	2–0

Fairly new to junior football, having been formed in 1956, Greenock Juniors had captured the imagination of the footballing public in Greenock and thousands of Greenock Morton fans were deserting the senior side to follow the Juniors. In the 1959/60 season this was understandable, as the 'big' side in Greenock had lost all six games in their league cup campaign, had been put out of the Scottish Cup in the first round by East Stirling, and had finished in fourteenth position in the second division.

In Greenock's replayed sixth-round tie against Johnstone Burgh, the attendance had been 13,200.

St Andrews United has also caused quite a stir by reaching the final, as they came from an area more interested in golf than football. Playing at outside left for them in the game that day was Romeo Borella, who had appeared in the 1957 final for Kilsyth but ended up on the losing side. On the way to Hampden, St Andrews had scored twenty-six goals but Borella failed to appear on the score sheet. That was all about to change; he became a two-goal hero for the Fifers. Formed in 1920, their best spell had been in 1926–29. They then experienced barren years until they won the Cowdenbeath Cup in 1958. The last team from Fife to have won the cup were Inverkeithing United, way back in 1913, when they defeated Dunipace 1–0.

The programme's front page had reverted back to the style of the 1958 final and showed head-and-shoulder photographs of Romeo Borella (St Andrews) and John Hogg (Greenock Juniors).

Headlines from 1960: Scotland was stunned by the news of another disaster befalling the nation. Nineteen firemen lost their lives while fighting a whisky warehouse blaze in Cheapside Street, Anderston Quay, Glasgow. The men never stood a chance as a 60-foot wall of the building fell on them and their fire appliances. Despite their shock at the loss of their colleagues, the other firemen continued to tackle the fire, which was eventually brought under control.
On television: *The Army Game*, *The Dickie Henderson Show*, *Candid Camera*.
On the radio: *Afternoon Theatre*, *In Touch*.
At the cinema: *The Magnificent Seven*, *Spartacus*.
Number one on 21 May: 'Cathy's Clown' by The Everly Brothers.

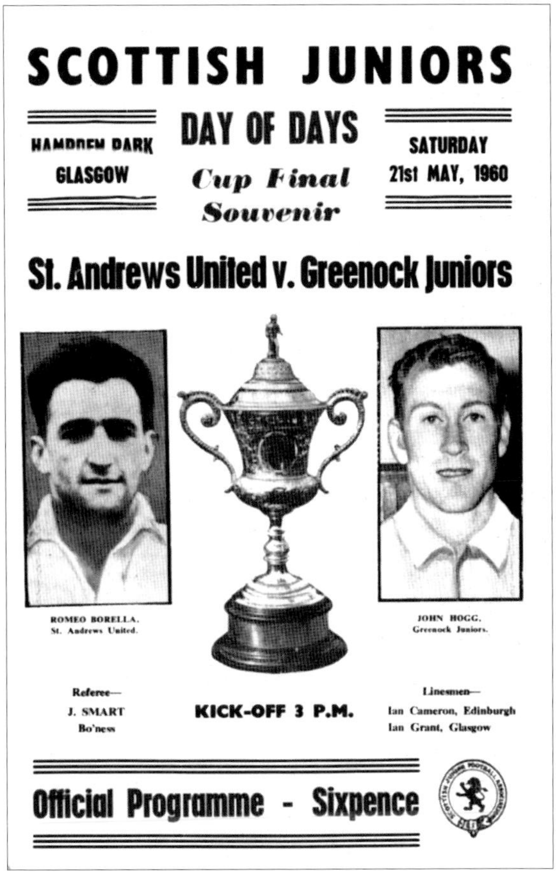

Right: The programme for the 1960 final.

Below: Captain John Hughes leads St Andrews onto Hampden Park.

St Andrews United at Hampden Park, 21 May 1960.

McKellar scores for Greenock Juniors.

Willie Penman scores St Andrews United's third goal.

Both sides congratulate each other at the final whistle.

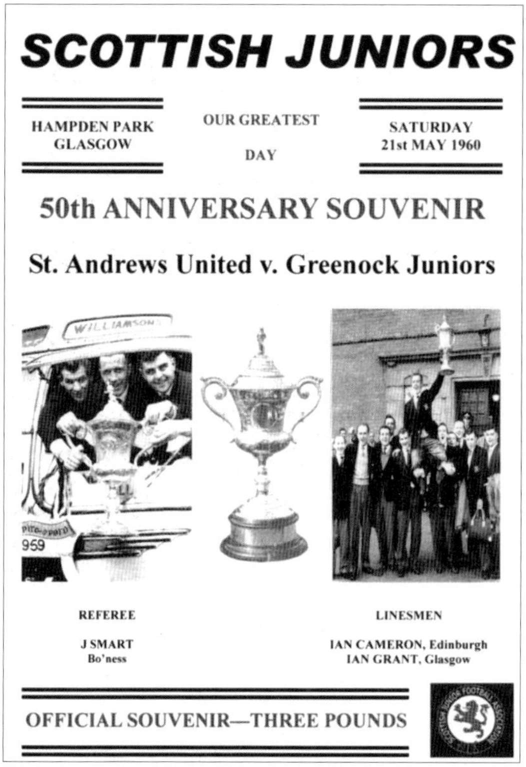

A fiftieth-anniversary souvenir published by the club in 2010.

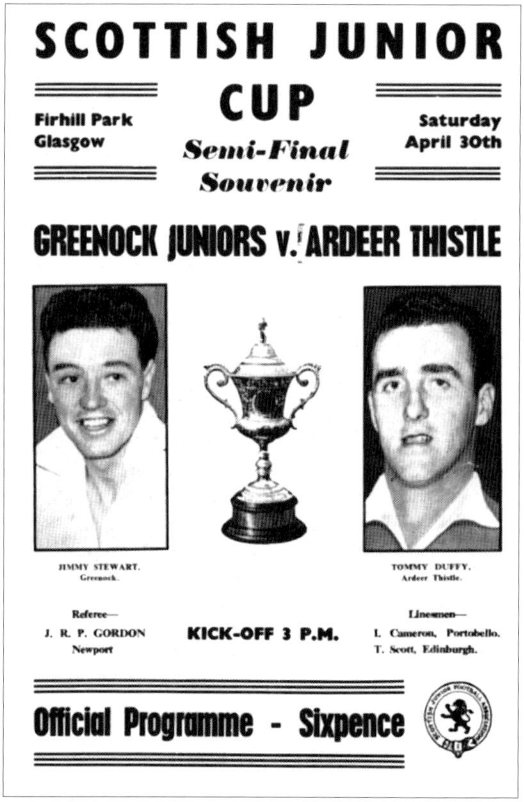

Programme for the 1960 semi-final at Firhill.

The programme for the 1960 semi-final at Stark's Park.

A programme for sixth-round tie, Thornton Hibs *v*. Blantyre Celtic.

HAMPDEN PARK
20 MAY 1961

Attendance: 20,000

Dunbar United 2 (Traynor, Craig)
Cambuslang Rangers 2 (Dickie, Thomson)

Dunbar United: Gillespie; Bellamy, Dunn; Howieson, Rae, Brown; Craig, Rennie, Meikle, Traynor, Gorman.
Cambuslang Rangers: Russell; Dawkins, Brown; Hosie, Dastey, Newlands; Friel, Thomson, Tees, Swan, Dickie.

Replay:
Dunbar United 2
Canmbuslang Rangers 0

Semi-finals: Dunbar United 3 Ashfield 2
Cambuslang Rangers 5 Dundee St Joseph 1

The Road to Hampden

Dunbar United		*Cambuslang Rangers*	
Linlithgow Rose (H)	2–0	Douglas Water Thistle (A)	6–1
Arniston Rangers (A)	3–2	St Anthony (A)	2–0
Bye	—	Beith Juniors (H)	6–2
Blairgowrie Juniors (H)	3–2	St Roch's (A)	4–3
Johnstone Burgh (H)	3–1	Ardrossan Winton Rovers (H)	3–0
Glenafton Athletic (A)	1–1	Camelon Juniors (H)	2–1
Glenafton Athletic (H)	1–1	Dundee St Joseph's (N)	5–1
Glenafton Athletic (N)	2–1		
Ashfield (N)	3–2		

Yet another David-against-Goliath scenario with Cambuslang very much the bookies' favourites. Dunbar, the small east-coast town, was noted more as a holiday resort with excellent golf courses than for its footballing deeds. Formed in 1928, the club was thought of as a 'Cinderella side'. This was their first ever appearance in a Hampden final.

By contrast, Cambuslang were a team packed with experience and already four of their players were provisionally signed with senior clubs. The match programme alluded to the number of players who had progressed to the senior ranks from Junior Football and listed the ex-Juniors presently with the Old Firm. It made interesting reading:

Rangers: Billy Ritchie, George Niven, Bobby Shearer, Eric Caldow, Davie Wilson, Alec Scott, Ralph Brand, Jim Baxter, Bobby Hume.

Celtic: Frank Haffey, Duncan MacKay, Jim Kennedy, Pat Crerand, Billy McNeil, John Divers, Bobby Carroll, John Hughes, Mike Jackson, John Clark.

Rangers had won the league that season and each of the players mentioned had played in the club's league campaign.

Headlines from 1961: Hollywood great Gary Cooper died just six days after his sixtieth birthday. He had been suffering from cancer and weeks before his death he was heavily sedated. John Wayne commented on the death of his friend, 'When Coop died a part of our business died with him.'

On television: *Coronation Street*, *The Russ Conway Show*, *Bootsie and Snudge*, *Harper West One*.

On the radio: *Afternoon Theatre*, *In Touch*, *Men from the Ministry*.

At the cinema: *The Guns of Navarone*, *Breakfast at Tiffany's*.

Number one on 20 May: 'Blue Moon' by the Marcels.

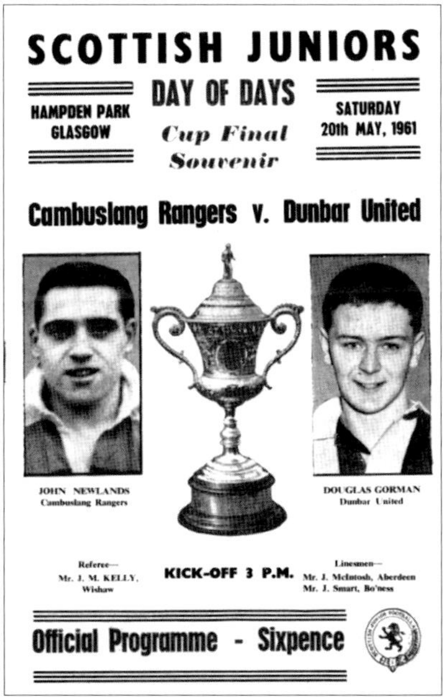

The programme for the 1961 final.

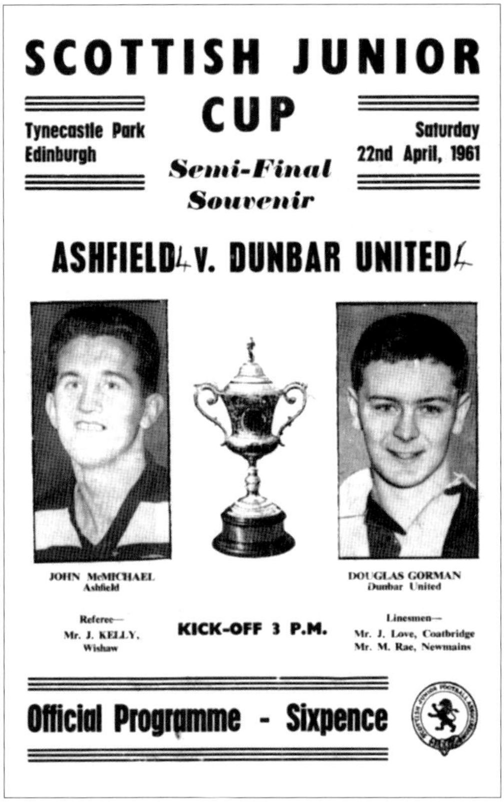

The programme for the 1961 semi-final at Tynecastle.

The programme for the 1961 semi-final at Muirton Park.

HAMPDEN PARK
19 MAY 1962

Attendance: 49,000

Kirkintilloch Rob Roy 1
Renfrew Juniors 1

Rob Roy: R. McLeod; Dyer, J. McLeod; Ferguson, Loughran, Cooper; Fascione, Knox, Fleming, McIlwraith, Cunningham.
Renfrew: Connelly; Collins, McMahon; Purdon, McDermid, McGrogan; McShee, Mowen, Rundell, Rooney, Newton.

Replay attendance: 19,500

Kirkintilloch Rob Roy 1
Renfrew Juniors 0

Semi-finals: Rob Roy 1 Glenafton Ath 0
Renfrew 4 Newburgh 0

The Road to Hampden

Kirkintilloch Rob Roy		*Renfrew Juniors*	
Kinnoul (A)	3–2	*Bye*	—
Dalry Thistle (H)	4–1	Vale of Clyde (H)	5–2
Tranent (H)	2–0	Dunbar United (A)	3–2
Petershill (A)	4–3	Saltcoats Vic (A)	2–2
Coltness United (H)	1–0	Saltcoats Vic (H)	7–3
Kilsyth Rangers (A)	2–2	Maryhill (H)	6–1
Kilsyth Rangers (H)	3–1	Greenock (H)	4–1
Glenafton Athletic (N)	1–0	Newburgh (N)	4–0

Formed in 1911, Renfrew had never won the cup and the last time they had appeared in the final was in 1917, when St Mirren Juniors had defeated them 1–0. They had been impressive on the way to the final stages, beating more fancied sides including the previous year's winners, Dunbar United.

Kirkintilloch Rob Roy, known as 'the Rabs', were one of the oldest Junior sides in Scotland – they had made their debut in 1894. This was their sixth time in the final, the first appearance being in 1906, which ended in a 1–0 defeat at the hands of Dunipace. In 1921 they won the trophy for the first time when they triumphed 1–0 over Ashfield. Rob Roy's next two appearances in 1932 and 1937 saw them lose 2–1 to Glasgow Perthshire and 5–1 to the Arthurlie, but they had a change of fortune in the 1943 final, defeating Benburb 3–1.

In Rob Roy's line-up the right-half was Martin Ferguson, the brother of Sir Alex. The following season Martin would go on to play for Partick Thistle and eventually he went into management.

The match programme made reference to the senior clubs advocating a Summer Cup competition in May and June. The Juniors were against this coming to fruition, as these months were looked upon as a time when they had the field to themselves, since the Senior season terminated in April.

From the outset of the season's competition all the teams were in the draw from the first round. Formerly the first three rounds were in the form of district eliminators.

Headlines from 1962: Glasgow said farewell to its tramcars. A quarter of a million people lined the streets as the 'caurs' made their final journey. Appropriately, the largest crowd had gathered at the junction of Hope Street and Argyle Street, near to the 'Heilanman's Umbrella', the area of Glasgow most associated with the trams. A part of Glasgow's life had come to a sad end.
On television: *Rawhide*, *The Bruce Forsyth Show*, *Maigret*, *The Bernard Delfont Show*.
On the radio: *The Men from the Ministry*, *Take your Partner*, *Go Man Go*.
At the cinema: *Dr No*, *Lawrence of Arabia*.
Number one on 19 May: 'Nut Rocker' by B. Bumble and the Stingers.

Above left: The programme for the 1962 final.

Above right: The programme for 1962 semi-final at Firhill.

The programme for the sixth-round tie, Newburgh *v.* Irvine Meadow.

HAMPDEN PARK
18 MAY 1963

Attendance: 21,384

Irvine Meadow 2 (Paterson, McIntyre)
Glenafton Athletic 1 (Moffat)

Irvine Meadow: Prentice; Miller, McVean; Dickie, Curran, Murray; Walker, Bingham, Garvie, McIntyre, Paterson.
Glenafton Athletic: Niven; Caldwell, McLean; Moffat, McKenzie, Murray; Maley, Brennan, Black, McCulloch, Paton.

Semi-finals: Irvine Meadow 3 Craigmark Burntonians 0
Glenafton Ath 3 Bonnyrigg Rose 2 (after 1–1 and 2–2 draws)

The Road to Hampden

Irvine Meadow		*Glenafton Athletic*	
Stonehaven (H)	6–0	Kirrie Thistle (H)	6–1
Blantyre Vic's (A)	6–1	Forth Wanderers (A)	4–0
Fauldhouse United (A)	2–1	Irvine Victoria (A)	6–0
Camelon (H)	6–1	Linlithgow Rose (A)	1–1
Dalkeith Thistle (A)	1–1	Linlithgow Rose (H)	2–0
Dalkeith Thistle (H)	5–1	Pollok (A)	1–0
Bellshill Athletic (H)	4–0	Cumnock (H)	5–0
Craigmark Burntonians (N)	3–0	Bonnyrigg Rose (N)	1–1
		Bonnyrigg Rose (N)	2–2
		Bonnyrigg Rose (N)	3–2

History was made when Irvine Meadow and Glenafton Athletic met in the finals. It was the first time that two Ayrshire sides had clashed in the last round. Five teams from Ayrshire had reached the last eight of the tournament that season: Irvine Meadow, Glenafton, Craigmark, Cumnock and Ardeer Recreation.

The Meadow were making their fourth appearance in a Hampden final, the previous one being in 1958/59 when they had overcome Shettleston 2–1. Four of their players from that day were in the team to play against Glenafton, namely Prentice, Dickie, Curran and Walker.

Glenafton Athletic of New Cumnock, who were formed in 1930, were in the final for the first time. They had been beaten semi-finalists the previous season, but Irvine Meadow were favourites to lift the cup. In Glenafton's line-up the centre-forward was Bobby Black, who had scored both goals for Shotts in the 1958 final. He had turned Senior with Airdrie but injury and illness had put him on the sidelines for a long spell. Black joined the Senior ranks once more when he signed for Third Lanark and gave the Hi Hi's two good seasons.

The programme carried advertisements for Burns & Laird Lines, Bank Restaurant in Queen Street, Glasgow (which was owned by former Celtic manager Willie Maley) and Cadet cigarettes, costing 3*s* 5*d* for twenty plain and 2*s* 10*d* for tipped.

The programme notes made reference to the harsh winter, which had resulted in a huge backlog of fixtures, both at Senior and Junior level. Consequently the season had been extended. As a result of this, attendances at Junior games had suffered badly.

Headlines from 1963: A massive police operation swung into action after the Glasgow-to-London mail train was robbed of what was thought to be in the region of £2 million by an organised gang. The train was halted by a fake signal near Cheddington, Buckinghamshire, and the train driver and his mate were overpowered. Fifteen men were later arrested for the crime and were given lengthy prison sentences.
On television: *Doctor Who*, *Steptoe and Son*, *Candid Camera*, *Dr Finlay's Casebook*.
On the radio: *Semprini Serenade*, *Take Your Partner*, *Treble Chance*.
At the cinema: *From Russia With Love*, *This Sporting Life*.
Number one on 18 May: 'From Me to You' by The Beatles.

Above left: The programme for the 1963 final.

Above right: The programme for the 1963 semi-final at Firhill.

Irvine's captain, John McIntyre.

HAMPDEN PARK
16 MAY 1964

Attendance: 49,115

Johnstone Burgh 1 (McGregor)
Cambuslang Rangers 1 (Kavanagh)

Johnstone Burgh: Carmichael; Wilson, McGregor; Dick, Greenwood, McEwan; Oliphant, Russell, Mallan, Tait, O'May.
Cambuslang Rangers: McLuskey; McKenzie, Hamill; Mitchell, Dastey, Kelly; Kavanagh, Collings, Young, Docherty, Johnstone.

Replay attendance: 23,000

Johnstone Burgh 3
Cambuslang Rangers 0

Semi-finals: Cambuslang Rangers 2 Irvine Meadow 0
Johnstone Burgh 3 Kirkintilloch Rob Roy 2

The Road to Hampden

Johnstone Burgh		*Cambuslang Rangers*	
Blantyre Vic's (H)	1–0	Cumnock (A)	3–2
Bye	—	Ardeer Recreation (H)	6–0
Whittletts Victoria (A)	4–3	Darvel (H)	4–2
Lochore Welfare (A)	4–3	Dunbar Utd (H)	4–3
Glenafton Athletic (H)	1–0	Port Glasgow (A)	2–0
Bonnyrigg Rose (A)	2–1	St Andrews Utd (A)	0–0
Rob Roy (N)	3–2	St Andrews Utd (H)	5–1
		Irvine Meadow (N)	2–0

This was Cambuslang's second visit to Hampden in four seasons; they had been beaten finalists in 1961. Their only cup win had been in 1937/38, when they defeated Benburb 3–2 in the final at Celtic Park. In their line-up for this final was John Dastey, who was Cambuslang's penalty expert and had missed only three penalty kicks out of the sixty he had taken. Dastey would go on to play for Cambuslang until 1970, making over 550 appearances.

In previous programmes for the final, the Junior FA referred to the Senior clubs extending their season and how it would have a detrimental effect on attendances at the Junior games.

At the end of 1963/64 season, all the Senior clubs apart from Rangers and Celtic took part in the newly introduced Summer Cup.

The SJFA's fears were ill-founded as, despite the extension to the senior season, attendances at Junior Cup ties had actually boomed and the match programme predicted a bumper gate inside Hampden. As it happened, the Summer Cup did not catch the imagination of the footballing public and it was discontinued after a couple of seasons.

Johnstone Burgh, only formed in 1956, were another side to reach the Hampden final for the first time. They were very much the underdogs in this clash, but as with previous finals the bookies got it wrong again.

The match programme made reference to the recent Scottish Cup final between Rangers and Dundee. Both sides had played all-out attacking football and had not adopted, as the notes said, 'the new fangled and stupid defensive 4–2–4 method'. Some Senior sides were experimenting with this style of play, which had been perfected by the Italians. Little did we know back then that all sorts of formations would be introduced to the game in the years to follow.

Headlines in 1964: The Beatles came to Glasgow amid scenes of mass hysteria. A crowd of over 8,000 was outside the Odeon Cinema in Renfield Street when the 'Fab Four' arrived and as the fans tried to break through the police cordon many hundreds fainted due to the crush. After the show The Beatles left by a side door, leaving thousands of fans still waiting outside.
On television: *It's Tarbuck*, *Crane*, *Star and Garters*, *The Avengers*.
On the radio: *Star Light Serenade*, *Saturday Club*, *Movie Time*.
At the cinema: *Mary Poppins*, *My Fair Lady*.
Number one on 16 May: 'Don't Throw Your Love Away' by The Searchers.

The programme for the 1964 final.

Jim Mallan, hat-trick hero for Burgh.

Johnstone Burgh, 1963/64 cup winners.

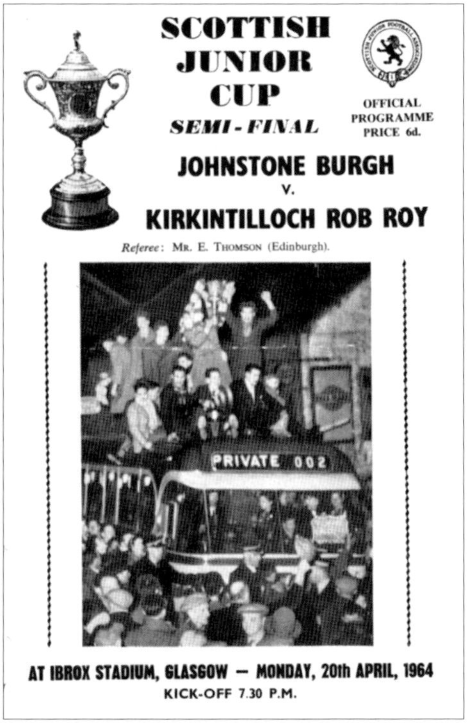

Above left: The programme for the 1964 semi-final at Firhill.

Above right: The programme for the 1964 semi-final at Ibrox.

HAMPDEN PARK
15 MAY 1965

Attendance: 35,000

Linlithgow Rose 4 (Oliphant, Grant, Cowie, Gardner)
Baillieston Juniors 1 (Traquair)

Linlithgow Rose: McGlynn; Reston, Syme; Veitch, J. Grant, Gardner; Henderson, C. Grant, Cowie, Fordyce, Oliphant.
Baillieston Juniors: Lindsay; Bryers, Crawford; McGuigan, Johnstone, McLure; Traquair, Moan, Black, Devine, Baxter.

Semi-finals: Linlithgow Rose 1 Kilsyth Rangers 0
Baillieston Juniors 4 Aberdeen Rosemount 0

The Road to Hampden

Linlithgow Rose		*Baillieston Juniors*	
Blantyre Vics (H)	4–0	*Bye*	—
Saltcoats Victoria (H)	4–3	Craigmark Burntonians (H)	2–1
Jeanfield Swifts (A)	2–1	Pumpherston (A)	2–2
Clackmannan (H)	3–0	Pumpherston (H)	2–1
Shettleston (H)	3–1	St Andrews (H)	3–1
Kilsyth Rangers (N)	1–0	Penicuik (A)	2–2
		Penicuik (H)	2–0
		Bellshill Athletic (H)	3–1
		Aberdeen Rosemount N)	4–1

The Royal and Ancient Burgh of Linlithgow is famous as the 1542 birthplace of Mary, Queen of Scots. But four centuries later it added another chapter to its illustrious history when Linlithgow Rose won the Scottish Cup at Hampden Park.

In years gone by, the residents of Linlithgow – known as 'Black Bitches' – had witnessed many a fine parade through its High Street as kings and queens and nobles of the royal court made their way to Linlithgow Palace. In his poem *Marmion*, Sir Walter Scott wrote:

Of all the palaces so fair,
Built for the royal dwelling,
In Scotland, far beyond compare,
Linlithgow is excelling.

However, the pomp and ceremony of those illustrious times paled into insignificance on that Saturday evening in May 1965 when Linlithgow Rose returned in triumph from Glasgow's Hampden Park amid scenes of great jubilation as thousands lined the famous old High Street to cheer the victors. All this might not have happened had it not been for the efforts made by the club's women's committee. At the start of the 1964/65 season, the Rose were almost penniless, but the women raised over £100 with various fundraisers, allowing the club to get over a difficult time. The team never looked back.

Opponents Baillieston had been admitted to the Junior ranks in 1919. They had only reached the final on one occasion, 1923/24, when they were defeated 3–1 by Parkhead at Firhill. They would have to wait another fifteen years before eventually winning the trophy in 1980.

The front cover for the match programme now showed an action photograph, although there was no indication as to which teams it referred. Advertisements were for Burns & Laird Lines, Red Hackle Scotch whisky, Sloan's Restaurant and Bank Restaurant. Our old friend the Laughing Cavalier was still in great shape on the back cover.

The centre pages contained the usual pen pictures of both sides. Celtic had won the Scottish Cup three weeks earlier and the programme notes made reference to the fact that all of the cup-winning team had stepped up from the Junior ranks – proving that the Juniors were an excellent recruiting source.

Headlines in 1965: Sir Winston Churchill passed away at the age of ninety-one. The man who had given Britain so much hope and inspiration during the dark days of the Second World War died in his sleep. A service held at St Paul's Cathedral was attended by heads of state from all over the world, including the Queen and other members of the royal family.
On television: *The Likely Lads*, *Peyton Place*, *The Power Game*, *The Royal Variety Show*.
On the radio: *I'm Sorry I'll Read that Again*, *Round the Horne*, *The World at One*.
At the cinema: *Dr Zhivago*, *Shenandoah*.
Number one on 15 May: 'Ticket to Ride' by The Beatles.

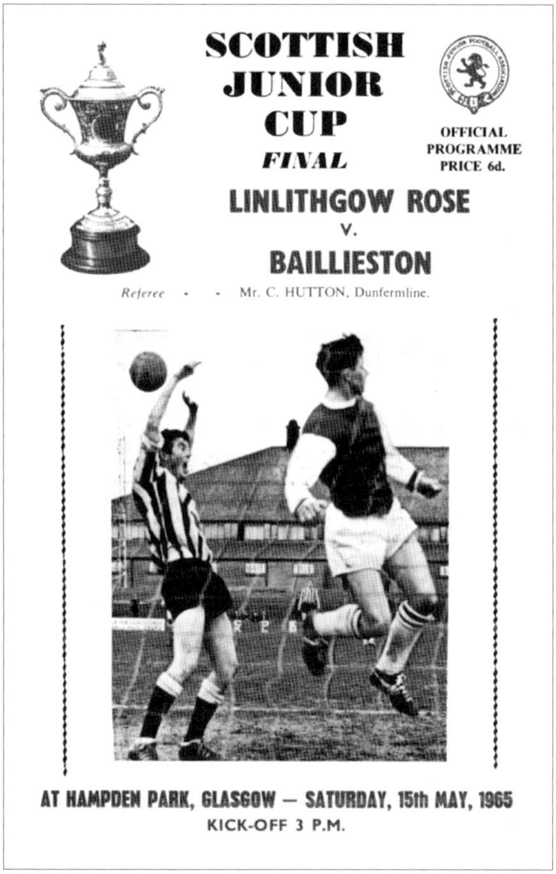

Right: The programme for the 1965 final.

Below: Lindsay, the Baillieston goalie, in action during the 1965 final.

Lindsay comes to the rescue once again.

Linlithgow laying siege to the Baillieston goal.

Linlithgow captain Tommy Reston is held high with the cup.

A group of happy Rose fans at Hampden Park.

Sporting handshakes at time-up.

Linlithgow Rose in 1965, with secretary David Roy on the back row, far right.

The programme for the 1965 semi-final at Muirton Park.

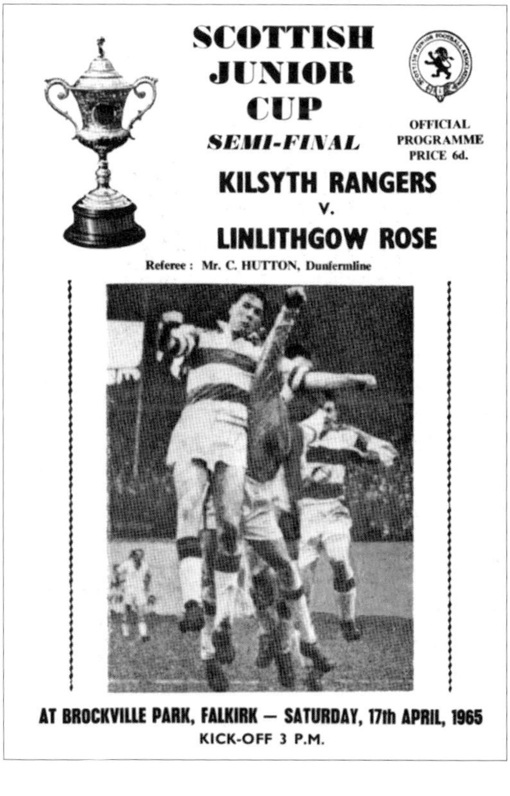

The programme for the 1965 semi-final at Brockville.

HAMPDEN PARK
21 MAY 1966

Attendance: 19,430

Bonnyrigg Rose 1 (Henderson)
Whitburn 1 (Penman)

Bonnyrigg Rose: McLeod; Young, Makarus; Henderson, Cattenach, Kelly; Wilson, Nisbet, Paterson, Davidson, Titterton.
Whitburn: Park; Stewart; Stevenson; McCallister; McIntyre; Muir; Murphy, Waddell, Sutherland, Halliday, Penman.

Replay attendance: 10,000

Bonnyrigg Rose 6
Whitburn 1

The Road to Hampden

Bonnyrigg Rose		*Whitburn*	
Dalkeith Thistle (H)	4–0	Preston Athletic (H)	3–1
Saltcoats Victoria (A)	1–0	Blantyre Vic's (H)	4–0
Broxburn Athletic (A)	6–1	St Roch (H)	2–0
Clackmannan (A)	4–1	Aberdeen Sunnybank (A)	2–0
Thorniewood Utd (H)	3–1	Armadale Thistle (H)	1–1
Aberdeen Rosemount (A)	2–0	Armadale Thistle (A)	2–1
Penicuik Athletic (N)	1–0	Beith (A)	4–2
		Shettleston (N)	1–0

This was the first all-east-of-Scotland final since Musselburgh Bruntonians met Arniston Rangers at the climax of the 1922/23 season. A big crowd was expected at Hampden.

As it transpired, it was the wettest Saturday for months and the attendance was under 20,000.

Bonnyrigg were by far the clear favourites for the replay, despite Whitburn's strong defence – a fact to which the match programme notes alluded to. However, Whitburn were dealt a massive blow when their top goal scorer and captain Danny Kilpatrick was ruled out of the replay with an injury.

Another wet evening for the game on the Wednesday night cut the attendance to 10,000. The Whitburn defence, which had stood firm throughout the cup campaign, crumbled in the face of Bonnyrigg's fire-power and the West Lothian side suffered the ignominy of being on the receiving end of the biggest defeat in a final in thirty-one years. Some match reports for the game suggested that the score-line flattered Bonnyrigg, but this was no consolation to Whitburn.

Over the years, many players who had worn Bonnyrigg's colours had gone on to greater things – John White and Pat Stanton to name but a few. But one former player went on to gain fame in movies – Thomas Sean Connery, better known as 007. 'Big Tam', as he was called in his earlier years, played with the Rose in the early 1950s and although he showed a lot of promise he decided to concentrate on his acting career.

The front of the cover showed an action shot from what appeared to be the 1961 final between Cambuslang Rangers and Dunbar United played at Hampden. It seemed a strange choice of photograph, but for the next seven years the front cover for semi-final and final programmes would show action shots from Senior and Junior games.

Headlines from 1966: Her Majesty The Queen Mother formally opened the new Tay Bridge linking Dundee with the Kingdom of Fife. The bridge, which took three years to build at a cost of £6 million, was over 7,000 feet in length and became Britain's longest road crossing over water. In Aberdeen, four men died on the construction site of the University of Aberdeen's new zoology department building. The tragedy happened when a seven-storey skeleton frame crashed to the ground, giving the men no chance of survival.
On television: *The Morecambe and Wise Show*, *Secombe and Friends*, *The London Palladium Show*, *Softly, Softly*.
On the radio: *The Joe Loss Pop Show*, *The Jimmy Young Show*.
At the cinema: *A Man For All Seasons*, *Alfie*.
Number one on 21 May: 'Pretty Flamingo' by Manfred Mann.

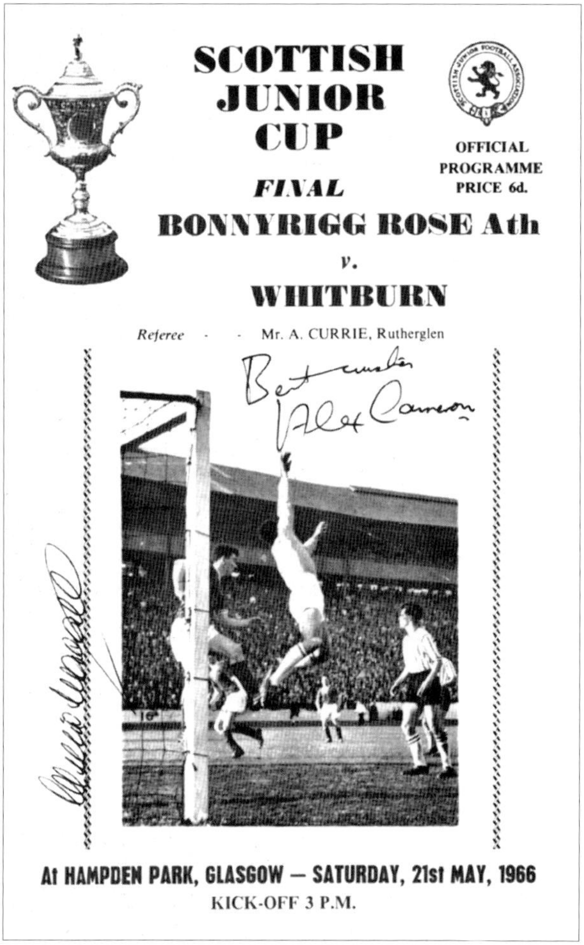

Left: The programme for the 1966 final.

Below: Bonnyrigg's second goal in the 1966 replay.

Penman scoring Whitburn's goal in the 6–1 defeat.

The Bonnyrigg Rose cup-winning side.

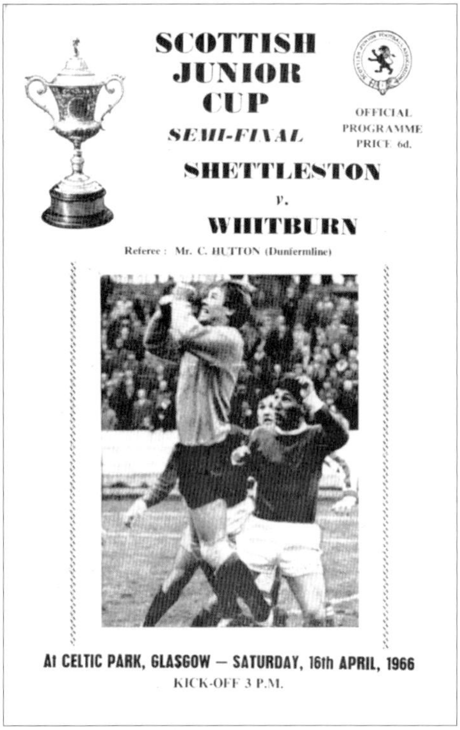

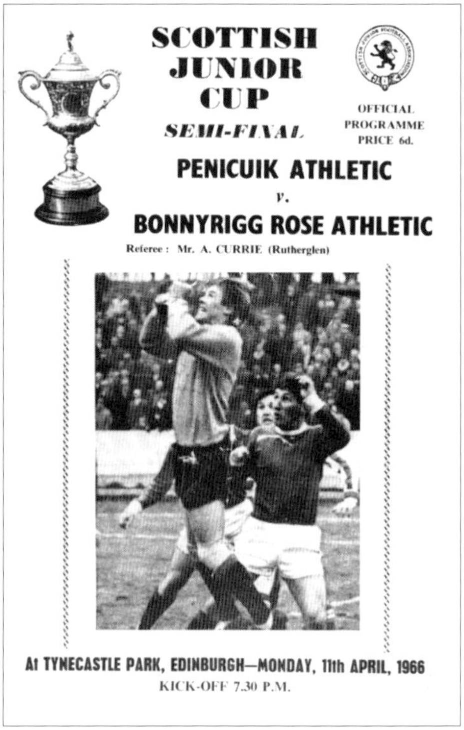

Above left: The programme for the 1966 semi-final at Celtic Park.

Above right: The programme for the 1966 semi-final at Tynecastle.

Wilson scoring for Bonnyrigg against Penicuik in the semi-final at Tynecastle.

A caricature of Sean Connery.

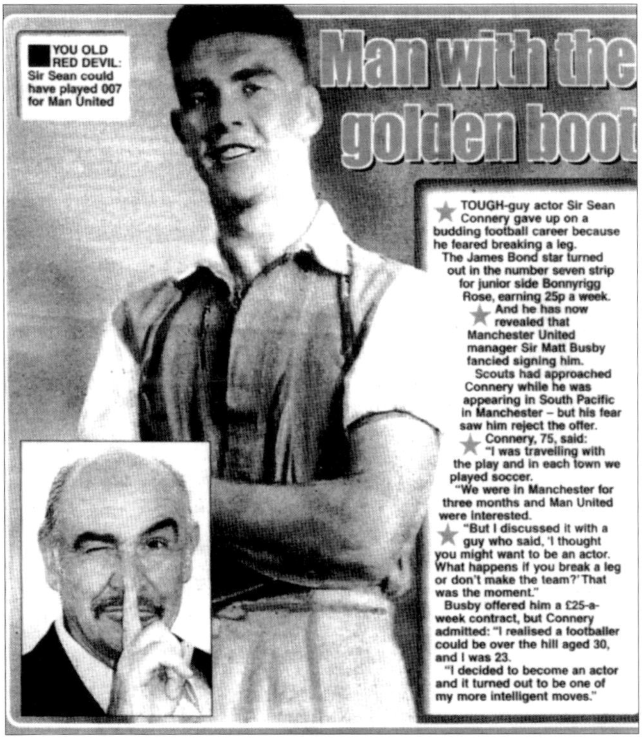

YOU OLD RED DEVIL: Sir Sean could have played 007 for Man United

Man with the golden boot

TOUGH-guy actor Sir Sean Connery gave up on a budding football career because he feared breaking a leg.

The James Bond star turned out in the number seven strip for junior side Bonnyrigg Rose, earning 25p a week.

And he has now revealed that Manchester United manager Sir Matt Busby fancied signing him.

Scouts had approached Connery while he was appearing in South Pacific in Manchester – but his fear saw him reject the offer.

Connery, 75, said: "I was travelling with the play and in each town we played soccer.

"We were in Manchester for three months and Man United were interested.

"But I discussed it with a guy who said, 'I thought you might want to be an actor. What happens if you break a leg or don't make the team?' That was the moment."

Busby offered him a £25-a-week contract, but Connery admitted: "I realised a footballer could be over the hill aged 30, and I was 23.

"I decided to become an actor and it turned out to be one of my more intelligent moves."

007 in Bonnyrigg's colours.

HAMPDEN PARK
20 MAY 1967

Attendance: 22,000

Kilsyth Rangers 1 (Wilson)
Rutherglen Glencairn 1 (McKay)

Kilsyth Rangers: Stewart; Fitzsimmons, McLaughlin; Grassan, Donnachie, Gordon; Carroll, McMahon, Paterson, Green, Wilson.
Rutherglen Glencairn: Phipps; Little, Brennan; Sutherland, Reid, Kennedy; McKay, Cowan, McGoldrick, Robson, O'Brien.

Replay attendance: 11,500

Kilsyth Rangers 3
Rutherglen Glencairn 1

Semi-finals: Kilsyth Rangers 4 Carluke Rovers 3
Rutherglen Glencairn 1 Johnstone Burgh 0 (after a 0–0 draw)

The Road to Hampden

Kilsyth Rangers		*Rutherglen Glencairn*	
Neilston (H)	7–1	*Bye*	—
Broxburn Athletic (A)	5–2	Maryhill (A)	0–0
Beith (H)	3–1	Maryhill (H)	2–0
Dundee St Joseph's (H)	2–0	Renfrew (A)	0–0
Glasgow Perthshire (A)	1–0	Renfrew (H)	4–1
Greenock (H)	4–4	Jeanfield Swifts (A)	2–0
Greenock (A)	4–1	Dundee Violet (H)	3–1
Carluke Rovers (N)	4–3	Vale of Leven (H)	1–0
		Johnstone Burgh (N)	0–0
		Johnstone Burgh (N)	1–0

A bit of history was made when substitutes were listed for the first time in a final. The Seniors had introduced substitutions at the start of 1966/67 season – Archie Gemmill being the first to be used when he replaced Jim Clunie for St Mirren in a game against Clyde at Shawfield.

It was a striking contrast with the previous season's east-of-Scotland final and it was a tribute to the Central League that their representatives had fought through to the last round to make it a west-of-Scotland clash.

The Glens had won the trophy on four previous occasions; their last victory had been in 1939 against Shawfield at Celtic Park. They had lost only two goals on the way to the final. However, their forwards had been less than convincing. By contrast, Kilsyth had notched up thirty goals and conceded twelve during their campaign.

As a result, the bookies couldn't agree on the outcome. It was no great surprise that it took a replay to settle the tournament.

In the programme notes, reference was made to Celtic and Rangers reaching the finals of the two major European competitions. A number of players from both sides' squads had come through the ranks of the juniors. Facing Inter Milan, Celtic had Auld (Maryhill Harp), Chalmers (Ashfield), Wallace (Kilsyth Rangers), Clark (Larkhall Thistle), Gallagher (Yoker Athletic), Gemmell (Coltness), Hughes (Shotts Bon Accord), Johnstone (Blantyre Celtic), Lennox (Ardeer Recreation) and McNeil (Blantyre Vics) in their squad. In the Rangers squad, against Bayern Munich, were Ritchie (Bathgate Thistle), Martin (Dalry Thistle), Johnston (Lochore Welfare), McKinnon (Dunipace) and Wilson (Baillieston).

Headlines from 1967: Two games of football grabbed the headlines. In April, Scotland beat World Cup holders England 3–2 at Wembley to the joy of the 20,000 travelling supporters. One month later, Celtic became European Champions and the first British team to win the trophy when they defeated Inter-Milan 2–1 in Lisbon.

On television: *Hogan's Heroes*, *The Golden Shot*, *The Prisoner*, *Ironside*.

On the radio: *Just a Minute*, *The World this Weekend*.

At the cinema: *Bonnie and Clyde*, *To Sir with Love*.

Number one on 20 May: 'Puppet on a String' by Sandie Shaw.

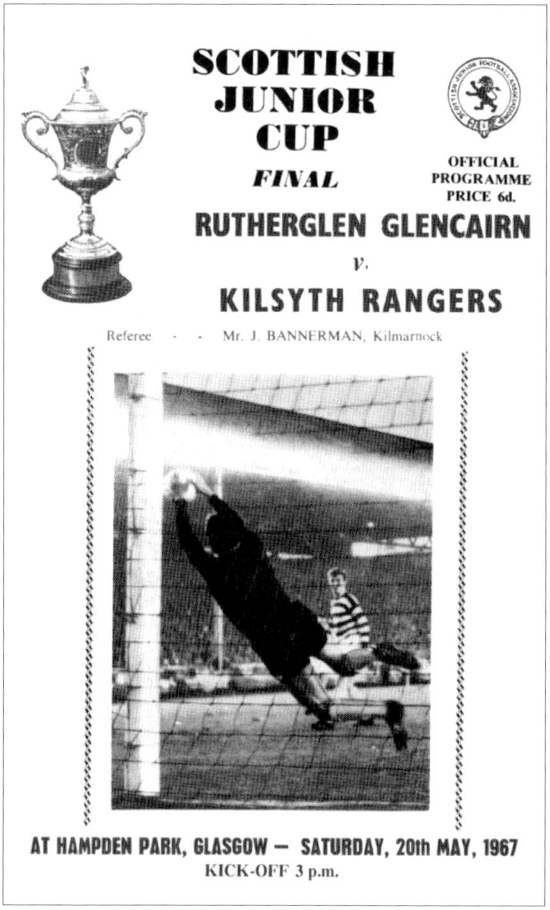

Left: The programme for the 1967 final.

Below: Kilsyth players and club officials in 1967.

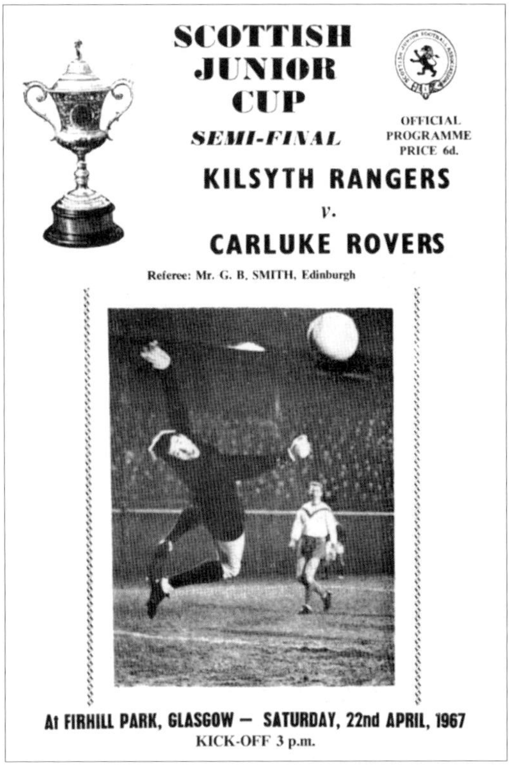

The programme for the 1967 semi-final at Firhill.

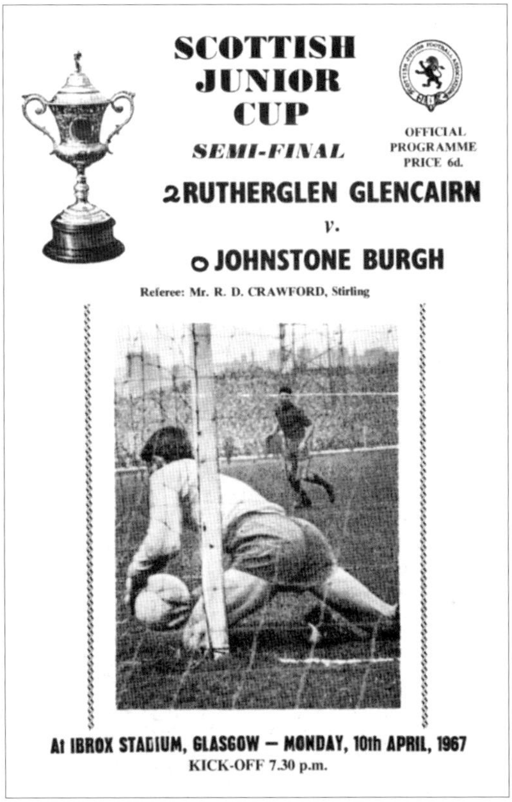

The programme for the 1967 semi-final at Ibrox.

HAMPDEN PARK
11 MAY 1968

Attendance: 28,700

Johnstone Burgh 2
Glenrothes 2

Johnstone Burgh: Connelly; Sturgeon, Caughey; Dick, Chisholm, House; Gilshan, Burke, McDonald, Reid, Boylan.
Glenrothes: Aird; Budd, Goodall; Forsyth, Nairn, Campbell; Downie, Johnstone, Goldie, Wood, Ross.

Replay attendance: 21,720

Johnstone Burgh 4
Glenrothes 3

The Road to Hampden

Johnstone Burgh		*Glenrothes*	
Newtongrange Star (H)	5–3	Jubilee Athletic	—*
Armadale Thistle (H)	4–0	Bankfoot Athletic (H)	8–1
Dunipace (A)	6–1	Luncarty (A)	4–0
Valleyfield Colliery (A)	4–1	Dundee Violet (A)	4–2
Cumbernauld United (A)	1–1	Linlithgow Rose (H)	5–1
Cumbernauld United (H)	2–2	Shotts Bon Accord (H)	1–1
Cumbernauld United (N)	1–0	Shotts Bon Accord (A)	2–1
Kilsyth Rangers (A)	2–2	Larkhall Thistle N)	4–0
Kilsyth Rangers (H)	3–2		
Lochee Harp (N)	3–2		

*Scratched

Since the 1964 final the front page of the programme had changed from showing the captains' photographs to depicting an action shot of a game. The programme for this final showed Jock Wallace, the Berwick Rangers goalkeeper, making a save against Rangers in the Scottish Cup match at Shielfield Park in January 1967, which Berwick won 1–0.

The price of a programme had been increased to a shilling, an increase of 100 per cent, but the layout was the same as in previous years. An advertisement for Johnnie Walker whisky was the centrepiece, with pen pictures of the teams on either side.

This was only Glenrothes' fourth season in junior football. They had formed in 1964, the year their opponents Johnstone Burgh had last won the trophy.

As the Senior side in Fife, Dunfermline Athletic had won the Scottish Cup by defeating Hearts 3–1 two weeks previously, so Glenrothes were hoping to make it a 'Fife Double' by lifting the Junior Cup.

Of the side that had triumphed in 1964, right-half Bobby Dick was the only remaining member in Johnstone's line-up against Glenrothes.

Headlines from 1968: The world of motor racing was stunned at the news of the death of world champion Jim Clark on Germany's Hockenheimring. Clark was driving a Formula 2 Lotus 48 in the Deutschland Trophäe when, on the fifth lap, he lost control at 170 mph on the wet and slippery track; the vehicle somersaulted several times before smashing broadside into a tree.
On television: *Dad's Army*, *Please Sir!*, *Nearest and Dearest*, *Life with Cooper*.
On the radio: *The Tony Blackburn Show*, *Nite Ride*, *Home this Afternoon*.
At the cinema: *Bullitt*, *The Yellow Submarine*.
Number one on 11 May: 'What a Wonderful World' by Louis Armstrong.

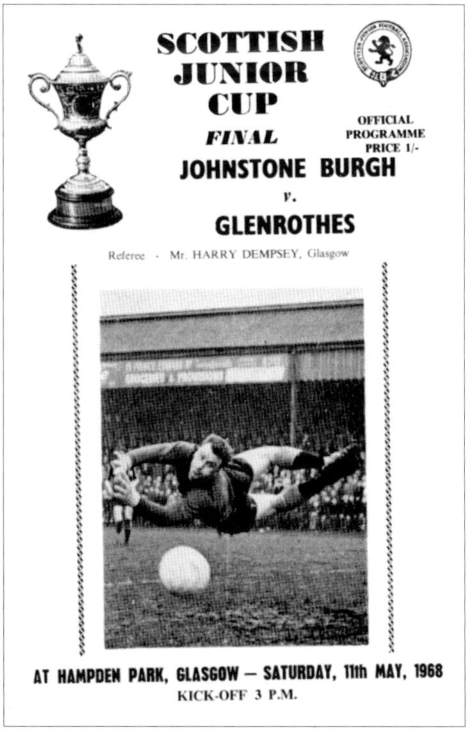

The programme for the 1968 final.

The programme for 1968 semi-final at Shawfield.

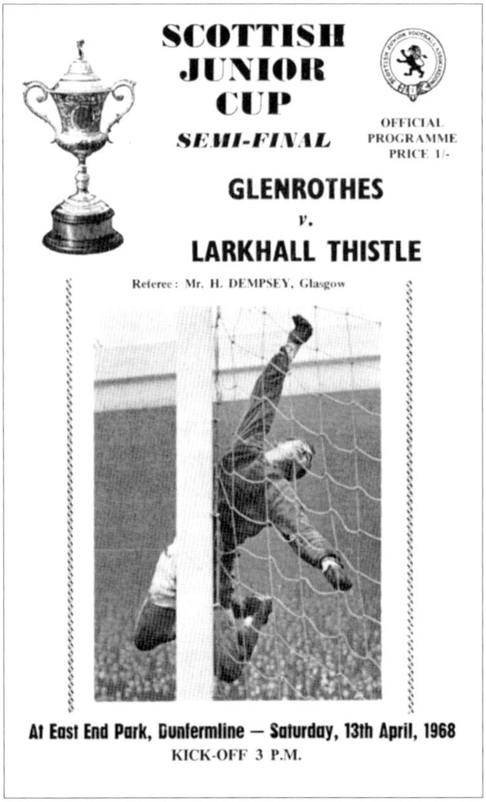

The programme for 1968 semi-final at East End Park.

HAMPDEN PARK
24 MAY 1969

Attendance: 32,524

Cambuslang Rangers 1 (Neilson)
Kirkintilloch Rob Roy 0

Cambuslang Rangers: Young; Pollock, Scullion; Letford, Gillespie, Nelson; Currie, McKenzie, Mathie, McCallum, Smith. Sub. Naismith.
Rob Roy: Eadie; Anderson, Johnstone; Walker, Craig, McCrae; Campbell, McLaren, McLean, Treacey, Ferguson. Sub. McCormack.

Semi-finals: Cambuslang Rangers 2 Irvine Meadow 1
Rob Roy 2 Linlithgow Rose 0

The Road to Hampden

Cambuslang Rangers		*Kirkintilloch Rob Roy*	
Bye	—	Royal Albert (A)	0–0
Port Glasgow (A)	2–2	Royal Albert (H)	3–1
Port Glasgow (H)	1–0	Larkhall Thistle (H)	4–3
Ashfield (A)	4–1	Lochore Welfare (H)	3–0
Carluke Rovers (A)	3–2	Bathgate Thistle (H)	2–2
St Andrews (H)	1–1	Bathgate Thistle (A)	3–2
St Andrews (A)	4–1	Armadale Thistle (H)	5–0
Glenrothes (H)	3–0	Cumnock (A)	3–1
Irvine Meadow (N)	1–1	Linlithgow Rose (N)	0–0
Irvine Meadow (N)	2–1	Linlithgow Rose (N)	1–1
		Linlithgow Rose (N)	2–0

The 1937/38 season was the last time that Cambuslang had won the trophy – by defeating Benburb 3–2. 1969 was the beginning of their love affair with the Scottish Junior Cup. They would appear in four of the next five finals, winning the trophy on three occasions. When they lost, it was only by a single goal scored from a penalty.

Kirkintilloch had been experiencing cash-flow problems in September of 1967 and had almost gone bankrupt. However, a new committee had been appointed and the club were transformed virtually overnight.

Each side had a good fanbase and a crowd of 30,000 was expected on the day.

In Cambuslang's line-up was Ross Mathie, who would go onto play for Kilmarnock and become a prolific goal scorer with the Ayrshire side.

Rob Roy's Billy McLaren had been provisionally signed by Dunfermline and after spells with the Fifers and Queen of the South he stepped into management with Stranraer, Queen of the South (twice), Hamilton Accies and Albion Rovers.

The photograph on the front of the match programme was the same one as had appeared three years earlier for the 1966 final.

Headlines from 1969: A gunman wanted in connection with the murder of an elderly woman in Ayr brought terror to the streets of Glasgow. James Griffiths opened fire on police officers and innocent bystanders from a house in Holyrood Crescent. A running battle then took place before Griffiths was shot and killed by armed police, but by then thirteen people, including a police officer and a twelve-year-old boy, had been wounded.
On television: *The Benny Hill Show*, *Please Sir!*, *Special Branch*, *The Dustbinmen.*
On the radio: *Ed Stewart*, *Waggoner's Walk*, *Scotch Corner.*
At the cinema: *Easy Rider*; *Butch Cassidy and the Sundance Kid.*
Number one on 24 May: 'Get Back' by The Beatles.

The programme for the 1969 final.

In stripes, Craig and Walker of Rob Roy challenge Mathie of Cambuslang.

Young, the Cambuslang goalkeeper, with the cup.

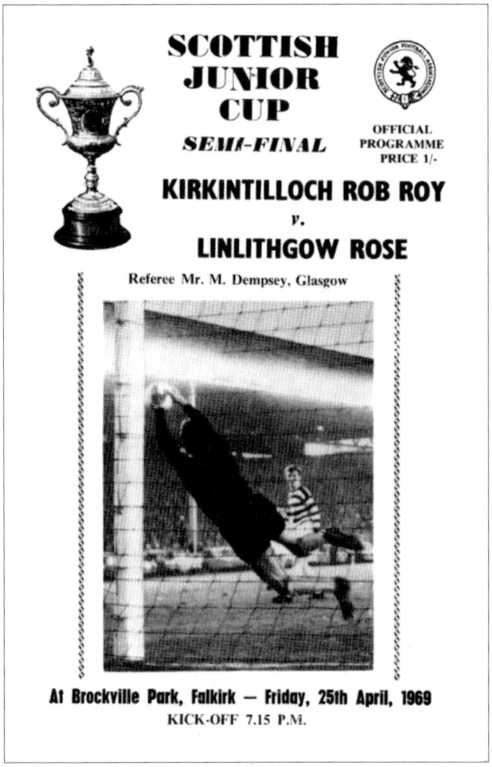

The programme for 1969 semi-final at Brockville.

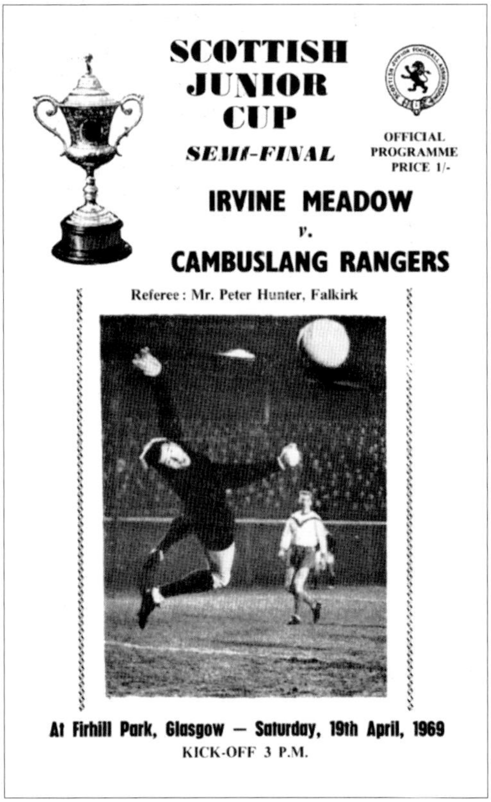

The programme for 1969 semi-final at Firhill.

HAMPDEN PARK
16 MAY 1970

Attendance: 19,500

Blantyre Victoria 1 (Lynn)
Penicuik Athletic 1 (Murphy)

Blantyre Vics: Watson; Thomson, Moore; Brodie, Douglas, Cunningham; Gallacher, McGrain, Lawson, Pickering, Lynn. Sub. Hemphill.
Penicuik Athletic: McDermott; Thorburn, McCabe; Hume, McGarry, Hogg; Robertson, Wallace, Stenhouse, Buchan, Finlayson. Sub. Murphy.

Replay attendance: 14,225

Blantyre Victoria 1
Penicuik Athletic 0

Semi-finals: Blantyre Victoria 2 Ardrossan 0
Penicuik Athletic 1 Ashfield 0

The Road to Hampden

Blantyre Victoria		*Penicuik Athletic*	
Bye	—	Tannochside Recreation (A)	3–1
Newtongrange Star (A)	3–1	Wishaw (H)	4–1
Shettleston (A)	1–1	Renfrew (H)	4–1
Shettleston (H)	1–0	Cumnock (H)	3–1
Whitburn (A)	1–0	Carluke Rovers (A)	0–0
Jeanfield Swifts (H)	2–1	Carluke Rovers (H)	1–1
Dalkeith Thistle (A)	1–1	Carluke Rovers (N)	2–1
Dalkeith Thistle (H)	1–0	Vale of Leven (A)	3–1
Ardrossan Winton N)	2–0	Ashfield (N)	1–0

Though it was back in 1888 that Penicuik Athletic first took to the football field, this was their first visit to Hampden for a Junior Cup Final. They were classed as the underdogs for this game, but they had talent aplenty in their side.

Goalkeeper Murray McDermott had already played at Senior level with Rangers and would again go Senior, with his career taking him to Raith Rovers, Berwick Rangers, Morton, Hearts (twice) and Meadowbank. McCabe, Stenhouse and Murphy had Senior experience with Hibs, Hearts and Notts County respectively.

Also in their ranks were Gordon Wallace and Malcolm Robertson, who were later transferred to Raith Rovers. Robertson went on to star with Ayr United and Hearts before signing for Toronto Blizzards. His son Sandy was later to play for Rangers and Coventry City in the 1990s.

Penicuik had already claimed the scalps of seven west-of-Scotland clubs on their way to Hampden, but there was to be no 'eightsome reel' on this occasion.

The tobacco giants John Player's sponsored the game and the winners were to receive £100 of football equipment and a Player's No. 6 trophy (the runners-up would take home £50). Penicuik had been the highest-scoring side in the competition and as a result would also receive £50 from Player's.

Headlines from 1970: Due to a dockers' strike, Scotland was in a frenzy as panic-buying by housewives left shops without commodities such as tinned fruit, sugar and bacon. Shops and supermarkets were packed as people stocked up and as a result rationing had already began in Dundee and Glasgow, with customers being limited to 4 lb of sugar at a time. In November there were chaotic scenes on the Kingston Bridge as ice caused dozens of minor accidents. This was the result of a year-long argument between Glasgow Corporation and the electricity board over the cost of the power required to run the in-built heating system that kept the bridge ice-free. The spate of accidents led to the matter being resolved.
On television: *The Eurovision Song Contest*, *On the Buses*, *A Family at War*, *Callan*, *Please Sir!*.
On the radio: *Album Time*, *Tony Blackburn in the Morning*.
At the cinema: *Kes*, *Ryan's Daughter*.
Number one on 16 May: 'Back Home' by the England World Cup Squad.

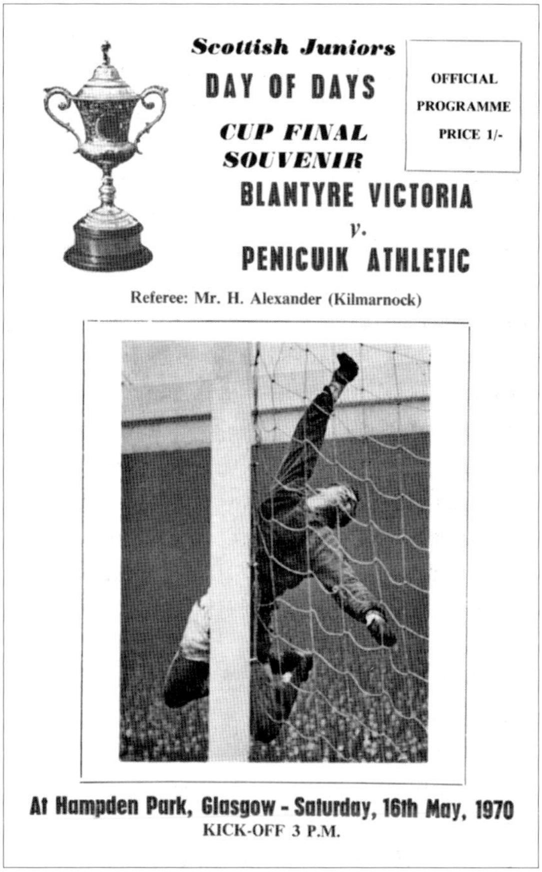

Right: The programme for the 1970 final.

Below: Buchan of Penicuik (in stripes) and Douglas of Blantyre in action.

Above: Blantyre Victoria, 1969/70 Scottish Junior Cup winners.

Left: Ardrossan's Watson saves against Blantrye in the 1970 semi-final.

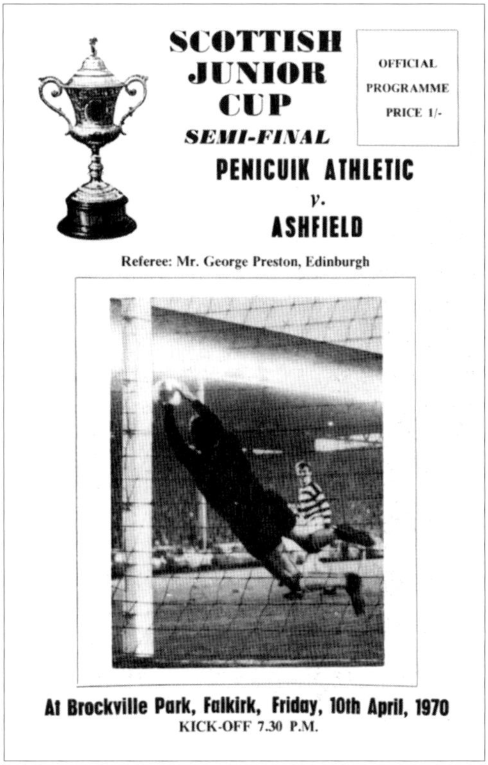

The programme for the 1970 semi-final at Brockville.

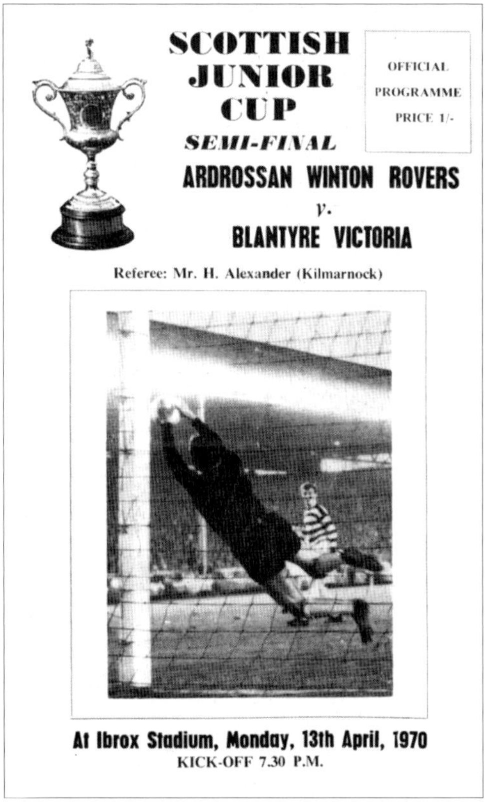

The programme for the 1970 semi-final at Ibrox.

HAMPDEN PARK
15 MAY 1971

Attendance: 24,676

Cambuslang Rangers 2 (Paterson, Neilson)
Newtongrange Star 1 (Stoddart)

Cambuslang Rangers: White; Sturgeon, Craig; Mordue, Scullion, McNeil; Lowrie, Cummings, Paterson, Nelson, McCallum. Sub. Gibson.
Newtongrange Star: Hogg; Knox, Printy; Sproull, Rennie, Gardner; Anderson, Hancock, Stoddart, Purcell, Hastie. Sub. Forrester.

Semi-finals: Newtongrange Star 3 Dalkeith Thistle 2
Cambuslang 1 Broxburn Athletic 0

The Road to Hampden

Cambuslang Rangers		*Newtongrange Star*	
Bye	—	Shotts Bon Accord (A)	1–1
Saltcoats Vics (A)	4–1	Shotts Bon Accord (H)	2–0
Errol (H)	3–1	Craigmark Burntonians (A)	5–2
Cumnock (A)	3–0	Vale of Leven (H)	3–0
Haddington (H)	5–1	Dundee North End (H)	1–0
Carluke (H)	2–2	Glenrothes (A)	2–1
Carluke (A)	2–0	Cumbernauld (H)	2–1
(Protested)	2–0	Dalkeith (N)	3 2
Broxburn Ath (N)	1–0		

Decimalisation had been introduced and the cost of the programme was now 5p, but the layout remained the same.

Sponsorship for the tournament had been introduced, with Drybrough Brewers and tobacco giants Player's to the fore

As a result, four pages of the eight-page programme carried advertisements for beer, whisky and cigarettes. Comments in the programme anticipated a crowd of 30,000.

Remarkably, only three players – Scullion, Nelson and McCallum – remained from the Cambuslang side of 1969.

Newtongrange Star – or 'Nitten' as they were known as locally – had last won the cup forty-one years previously, when they had defeated Aberdeen's Hall Russells 3–0 at Tynecastle.

Over the years they had produced many footballers who went on to greater things, Dave McKay (Hearts and Spurs), Alex Young (Hearts and Everton), Mike Haughney (Celtic) and Walter Kidd (Hearts) to name but a few. In the team for the final was Steve Hancock, who would progress to play with Celtic and Hearts.

Headlines from 1971: Two major disasters stunned the nation. On 2 January, sixty-six people were killed and over 140 injured in what has come to be known as the Ibrox Disaster. At the end of a fairly quiet Old Firm game that had ended in a 1–1 draw, tragedy struck at Stairway 13 situated at the east end of the ground. It was a popular exit for Rangers fans as it was nearest to the supporters' buses and the Ibrox subway. As a result, it was densely packed with supporters. It is thought that someone at the top of the stairway tripped or that some people stumbled on the way down, but whatever the reason a 'domino' effect took place and the crowd toppled and collapsed. Very quickly and with no means of escape, people were heaped on top of each other and crushed to death. In October, a massive mid-afternoon gas explosion destroyed a shopping centre in Clarkston near Glasgow. Twelve people were killed and dozens more were injured as premises collapsed within the shopping complex.
On television: *The Benny Hill Show*, *Bless this House*, *The Persuaders*, *Man at the Top*, *Sports Night with Coleman*.
On the radio: *The Long March of Everyman*, *Words*.
At the cinema: *A Clockwork Orange*, *Dirty Harry*.
Number one on 15 May: 'Brown Sugar' by The Rolling Stones.

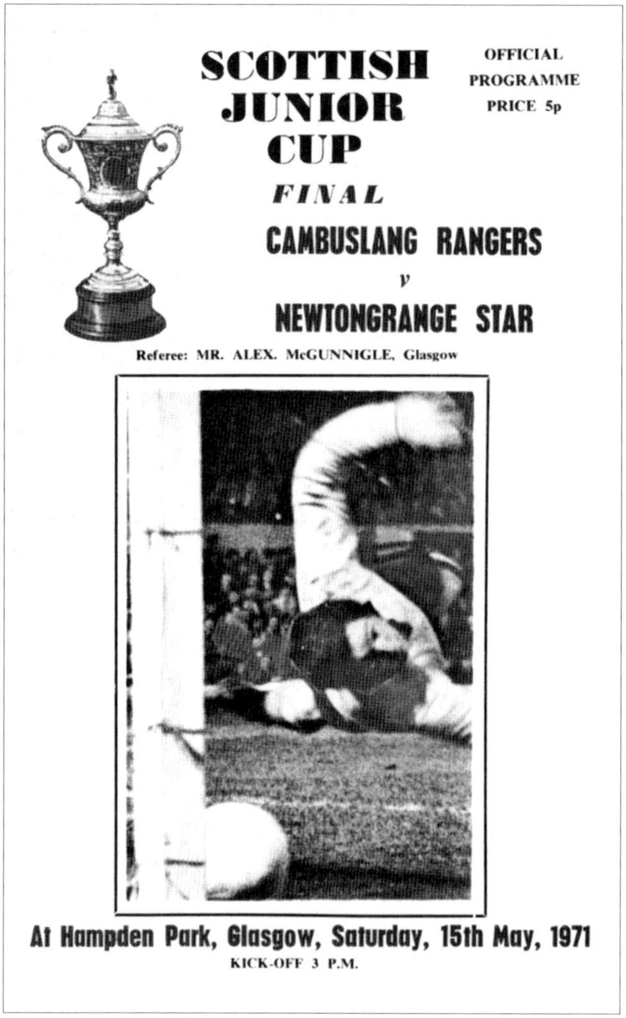

Left: The programme for the 1971 final.

Below: Cambuslang Rangers at Hampden for the 1971 final.

Billy Paterson scoring the equaliser against Newtongrange.

Keith Nelson scoring the winning goal for Cambuslang.

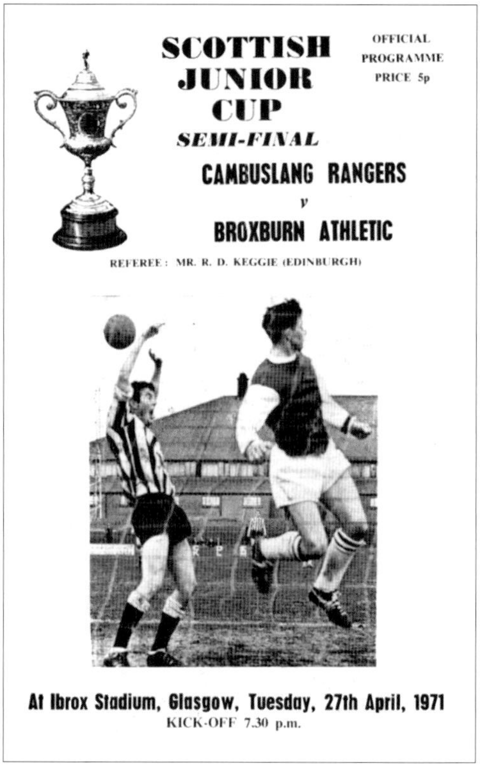

The programme for the 1971 semi-final at Ibrox.

The programme for the 1971 semi-final at Easter Road.

HAMPDEN PARK
3 JUNE 1972

Attendance: 20,000

Cambuslang Rangers 1 (Cummings)
Bonnyrigg Rose 1 (Ford)

Cambuslang: White; Gallagher, Brown; Murphy, Mordue, Lowrie; Nelson, Thomson, Cummings, Paterson, McCallum. Sub. Sturgeon, Russell
Bonnyrigg Rose: Ferguson; Young; Hume; McIver, Begbie, Matear; McQueen, Porter, Ford, Henry, Earl. Sub. Moore, Gowans.

Replay attendance: 14,000

Cambuslang Rangers 3
Bonnyrigg Rose 2

Semi-finals: Cambulang Rangers 3 Johnstone Burgh 0
Bonnyrigg Rose 1 Newtongrange Star 0

The Road to Hampden

Cambuslang Rangers		*Bonnyrigg Rose*	
Bye	—	Annbank Utd (H)	3–1
Dunbar Utd (H)	1–1	Vale of Clyde (H)	6–3
Dunbar Utd (A)	2–0	Royal Albert (A)	3–1
Formartine Utd (A)	1–1	Blantyre Celtic (A)	1–1
Formartine Utd (H)	9–0	Blantyre Celtic (H)	5–1
Armadale Thistle (H)	5–0	Rob Roy (H)	1–0
Yoker Athletic (H)	2–1	Vale of Leven (A)	2–1
Kello Rovers (H)	6–1	Newtongrange Star (N)	1–0
Johnstone Burgh (N)	3–0		

Cambuslang Rangers were hoping to win the trophy for the second season in succession – a feat last achieved by Ashfield in 1895.

They were a vastly experienced side comprised mostly of players who had honed their skills at Senior level and there had only been four changes of personnel since the previous year's final. By comparison, Bonnyrigg were a young side who had been dealt a huge blow by the loss of their top scorer, George Dixon, prior to the final. In right-back Archie Young they had the only surviving member of their 1966 Junior Cup win.

In the match programme notes, a crowd of 30,000 is anticipated; it fell well short. The front page carried a photograph of Glasgow Rangers in action at Ibrox Stadium, with Colin Jackson of Rangers in the background.

Headlines from 1972: In Barcelona in May, Rangers defeated Moscow Dynamo 3–2 to bring the Cup Winners' Cup to Glasgow. It was a splendid achievement by the Ibrox Club but the victory was overshadowed by the Spanish police attacking the Rangers supporters that had come onto the field at the end of the game to celebrate. Nonetheless, two days later, the victorious team paraded the cup round Ibrox Stadium in front of over 20,000 fans.
In September, the world was shocked to learn that eight Israeli Olympic athletes who had been taken hostage by Arab terrorists had been killed as West German police tried to rescue them from their captors. The athletes had been taken hostage from the team's quarters at the Games Village in Munich.
On television: *Till Death Us Do Part*, *Public Eye*, *Bless this House*, *On the Buses*.
On the radio: *I'm Sorry I Haven't a Clue*, *The Last Goon Show of All*.
At the cinema: *The Godfather*, *Last Tango in Paris*.
Number one on 3 June: 'Metal Guru' by T. Rex.

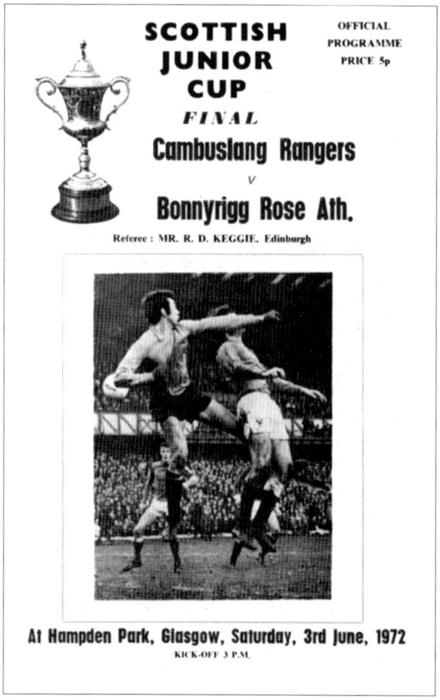

The programme for the 1972 final.

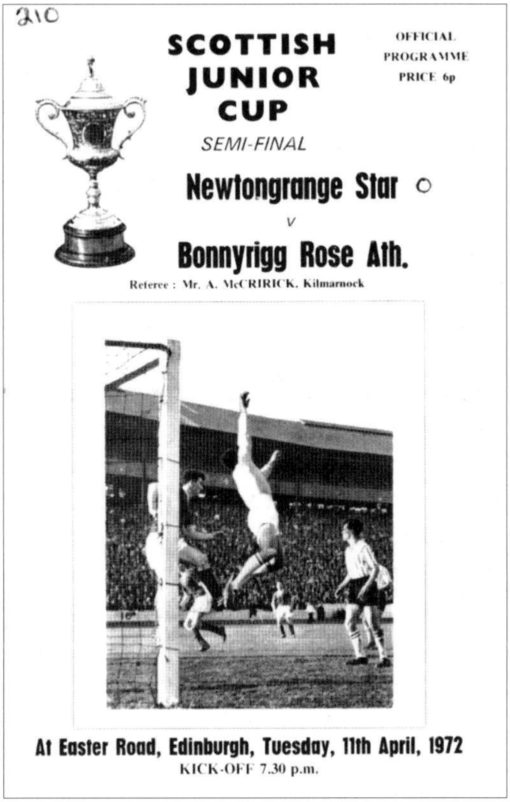

The programme for the 1972 semi-final at Easter Road.

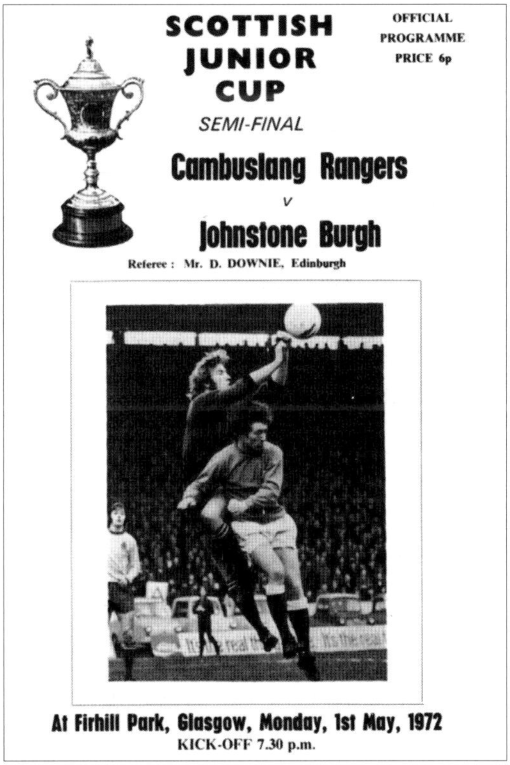

The programme for the 1972 semi-final at Firhill.

Cambuslang Rangers at Hampden Park for the 1972 final.

Bonnyrigg keeper Ferguson sees the ball past the post.

Ferguson saves after an attack by the Cambuslang forwards.

Cummings turns away after scoring for Cambuslang.

HAMPDEN PARK
28 APRIL 1973

Attendance: 22,242

Irvine Meadow 2 (Johnstone, Morris)
Cambuslang Rangers 2 (Cummings 2)

Irvine Meadow: Hay; Short, Renfrew; McCrorie, Bashford, O'Brien; Hume, Johnstone, Gillespie, McLaughlin, Morris. Sub. Pinkerton, Lewis.
Cambuslang Rangers: White; Rothwell, Brown; Thomson, Mordue, Lowrie; McQuade, Paterson, Cummings, Craig, McCallum. Sub. Brock, Telford.

Replay attendance: 24,917 (after another draw, this time 3–3)

Irvine Meadow 1
Cambuslang Rangers 0

Semi-finals: Cambuslang 4 Newburgh 0
Irvine Meadow 4 East Kilbride 1

The Road to Hampden

Irvine Meadow		*Cambuslang Rangers*	
Bye	—	Neilston (H)	2–0
Haddington Athletic (A)	2–2	Rob Roy (A)	2–2
Haddington Athletic (H)	1–1	Rob Roy (H)	4–0
Haddington Athletic (N)	2–0	Cumbernauld Utd (H)	2–1
Bonnyrigg Rose (A)	3–1	Arbroath Victoria (H)	4–1
Kilsyth Rangers (H)	4–1	Dundee Osborne (H)	4–0
Lochore Welfare (H)	3–3	Newburgh Athletic (N)	4–0
Lochore Welfare (A)	1–0		
Linlithgow Rose (A)	3–3		
Linlithgow Rose (H)	3–1		
East Kilbride Thistle (N)	4–1		

Cambuslang Rangers were all set to create a record by winning the cup for an unprecedented third time in successive competitions. They had made only four changes in personnel since the 1971/72 final. Cambuslang were managed by Davie McLaggan, who had recently been appointed the first ever team manager of Junior Scotland in recognition of his sterling work.

The Scottish Juniors had defeated their English counterparts 5–1 a few weeks previously and three of the team – Mordue, Cummings and McCallum – had been supplied by the 'Wee Rangers', so it was no surprise that the bookies viewed them as hot favourites to lift the trophy once again, given their vast experience. Cambuslang, apart from a hiccup at Kirkintilloch, had swept into the final stages in some style. Irvine Meadow, on the other hand, had been involved in four replayed games before securing the final place. Both sides were known for their attacking style, so a great game of football was anticipated. As it transpired, a third game was necessary to settle the outcome.

As both teams normally played in royal blue, Irvine Meadow turned out in red for the occasion and Cambuslang changed to white.

The front page of the programme showed an action shot from the previous year's final between Cambuslang and Bonnyrigg. The inside contained the usual advertisements for alcohol and cigarettes

Headlines from 1973: The nation was in the grip of a fuel crisis caused by a train drivers' strike and a ban on miners' overtime. The strike and overtime ban together threatened to dispute the movement of coal to power stations and industries. To add to the Government's woes, Glasgow's firemen went on strike over their salaries and working conditions. The strike lasted eight weeks; the firemen were awarded a wage increase.
On television: *Colditz*, *Van der Valk*, *Some Mothers Do 'Ave 'Em*, *Cilla*.
On the radio: *The Radio Roadshow*, *The Story of Pop*, *Checkpoint*.
At the cinema: *The Day of the Jackal*, *The Sting*.
Number one on 28 April: 'Tie a Yellow Ribbon Round The Ole Oak Tree' by Dawn featuring Tony Orlando.

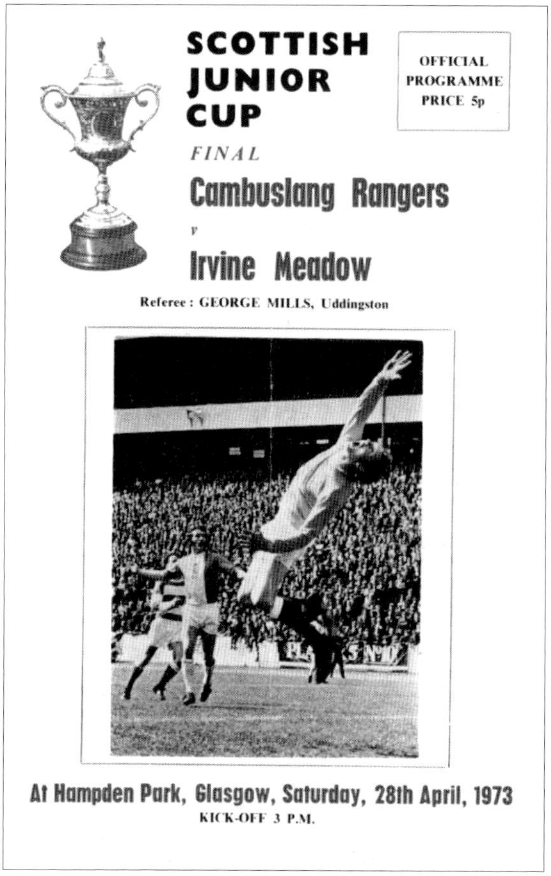

Left: The programme for the 1973 final.

Below: The 1972/73 winners' medal, this one owned by Con Renfrew.

The reverse of Con Renfrew's medal.

Irvine Meadow, Scottish Junior Cup winners 1972/73.

The Cambuslang Rangers line-up at Hampden Park in 1973.

Cummings scoring for Cambuslang in the 1973 final.

Morris scores for Irvine in the 1973 replay.

Cummings of Cambuslang equalising in the 1973 replay.

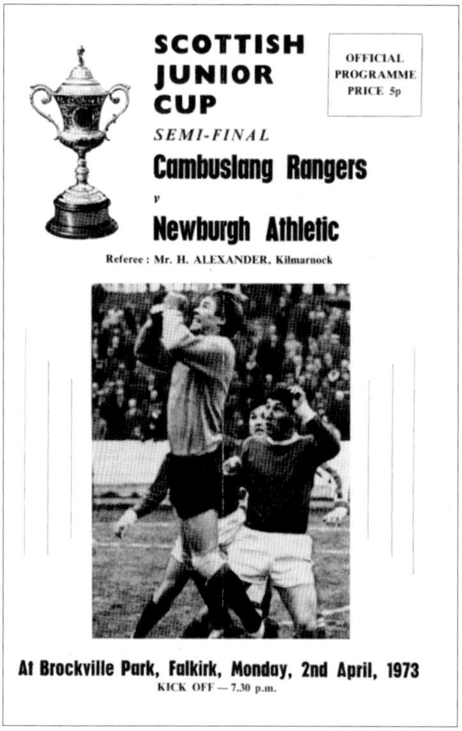

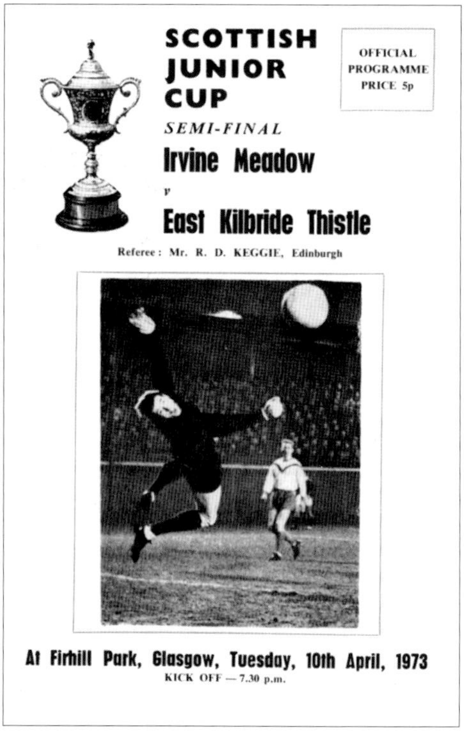

Above left: Programme for the 1973 semi-final at Brockville.

Above right: Programme for the 1973 semi-final at Firhill.

Irvine's Gillespie scoring in the semi-final against East Kilbride.

HAMPDEN PARK
27 APRIL 1974

Attendance: 22,830

Cambuslang Rangers 3 (Morrison, Cummings 2)
Linlithgow Rose 1 (Steele)

Cambuslang Rangers: Orr; Morrison, Brown; Mordue, Reid, Ferguson; Cummings, Thomson, Paterson, Craig, McCallum. Sub. Brannigan, McLaughlin.
Linlithgow Rose: Donaldson; McCann, Ure; Steele, Frew, Cruickshanks; McCaffer, McMeechan, Donald, Wilson, Halliday. Sub. Cairns, McPherson.

Semi-finals: Cambuslang Rangers 2 Glasgow Perthshire 0
Linlithgow Rose 3 Blantyre Vics 0

The Road to Hampden

Cambuslang Rangers		*Linlithgow Rose*	
Bye	—	*Bye*	—
Bathgate Th (A)	6–2	Penicuik Ath (A)	0–0
East Kilbride (H)	2–2	Penicuik Ath (H)	3–0
East Kilbride (A)	2–2	Glenafton Ath (H)	5–0
East Kilbride (N)	5–4	Blairgowrie (A)	0–0
Greenock Juniors (H)	3–1	Blairgowrie (H)	2–1
Musselburgh Ath (H)	2–0	Stonehaven (H)	4–1
Glenrothes Juniors (H)	5–2	Petershill (H)	3–0

Cambuslang had won the cup two years previously for the second time in succession and had been finalists in 1973, when they had been denied the record of winning three Junior Cups in a row – something that had not happened in the history of the competition. Because of their previous record and the vast experience in their ranks, the bookies ranked Cambuslang as clear favourites for the trophy. By contrast, Linlithgow's last final appearance had been 1965, when they had defeated the much-fancied Baillieston Juniors. This time the bookmakers were proved correct.

Cambuslang had now won the trophy for the fifth time and by doing so became only the third club in the Junior Cup's history to achieve such a feat, the other two being Petershill and the now-defunct Parkhead Juniors.

The programme for the match had been completely re-vamped and two extra pages had been added, but the price remained 5p. The centrepiece of the front cover carried the logo of the Scottish Junior Football Association, replacing the action shots shown in previous programmes. Photographs of both teams were produced inside and altogether the programme carried a bit more information, although advertisements for cigarettes, beer and whisky still took up the back and middle pages.

Headlines from 1974: A general election for 28 February was called for by Prime Minister Edward Heath after the National Union of Mine Workers decided to a national strike from 9 February. The row had been simmering for some time and a pithead ballot of 81 per cent voting for industrial action sealed the decision to strike.
The Scottish based oil company Burmah announced in April that it had made the biggest discovery yet of North Seas oil and predicted that production could reach 900,000 barrels a day. Celtic completed 'Nine in a Row' wins in the League Championship and completed the double by defeating Dundee United 3–0 in the Scottish Cup Final.
Red Rum won the Scottish Grand National at Ayr.
On television: *Porridge*, *Rising Damp*, *Harry O*, *The Waltons*, *Tiswas*.
On the radio: *Sounds of Scotland*, *The World Tonight*.
At the cinema: *The Conversation*, *The Godfather Part II*.
Number one on 27 April: 'The Cat Crept In' by Mud.

The programme for the 1974 final.

Morrison gives Cambuslang the lead with a successful penalty in the 1974 final.

Cummings of Cambuslang scores the second goal.

Cummings, the two-goal hero, is lifted up by his teammates.

Above left: The programme for the 1974 semi-final at Firhill.

Above right: The programme for the 1974 semi-final at Brockville.

Linlithgow Rose in 1974.

Cambuslang Rangers in 1974.

The semi-final at Brockville sees Donald of Linlithgow Rose scoring against Blantyre Victoria.

In the other semi-final at Firhill, Brown of Cambuslang scores with a penalty.

HAMPDEN PARK
26 APRIL 1975

Attendance: 17,776

Glenrothes Juniors 1 (Cunningham)
Rutherglen Glencairn 0

Glenrothes: Cooper; White, Baker; Dair, McKenzie, Duncan; Cunningham, Judge, McInnes, Thomson, Walker. Sub. Jack, Hynd.
Rutherglen Glencairn: Ward; Spiers, McManus; Carracher, Roberts, Reid; Mullaney, McDonald, Evans, Dickson, Woods: Sub. McMillan, McGrannigan

Semi-finals: Glenrothes 3 Ashfield 0
Rutherglen 3 Kilbirnie Ladeside 2

The Road to Hampden

Rutherglen Glencairn		*Glenrothes*	
Haddington (A)	5–1	*Bye*	—
Forres Thistle (H)	6–0	Arbroath Vic (H)	3–1
Lewis Utd (A)	2–1	Dunipace Juniors (H)	4–1
Larkhall Thistle (H)	2–1	St Roch's (H)	1–0
Petershill (H)	2–2	Cumbernauld (H)	2–0
Petershill (A)	1–0	Baillieston (H)	2–2
Kello Rovers (H)	1–0	Baillieston (A)	1–0

It was hailed as 'the Battle of the Glens' as both sides were affectionately known to their followers as 'the Glens'.

Rutherglen Glencairn's name first appeared on the Junior Cup in 1901/02 after they had defeated Maryhill 1–0. They were again victorious in 1918/19, 1926/27 and 1938/39.

Glenrothes were still regarded by some as a 'fledgling team' having only been formed in 1964. This was despite the fact that four years after being founded they had reached the final in 1968, when they were narrowly defeated by Johnstone Burgh. An interesting point about the game was that Hugh McKay and John

Forsyth, the respective team managers, had played for their clubs when they last appeared in the final – Hugh McKay for Rutherglen in 1967 and John Forsyth for Glenrothes the following year. The match was sponsored by tobacco giants John Player & Sons.

The programme contained photographs of both sides and action shots from the respective semi-finals. It now cost 10p.

Headlines from 1975: There was a call for action when employment figures revealed that over a million were unemployed in the UK. The STUC and the Scottish Labour Party wanted a special employment agency set up with Government backing to begin training schemes and special projects to assist jobless youngsters. In March there was still no end to the lengthy strike by Glasgow's dustcart drivers and the Government decided to use the Army to clear up the backlog of rubbish for fear of rodents infesting the city. Meanwhile, Rangers ended Celtic's dominance of Scottish football by winning the League Championship courtesy of a Colin Stein equaliser against Hibs at Easter Road on 29 March. It was the Ibrox club's first league title in eleven years.
On television: *The Two Ronnies*, *Starsky and Hutch*, *Bless This House*, *Open All Hours.*
On the radio: *A Good Read*, *You the Jury*, *Quote... Unquote.*
At the cinema: *Dog Day Afternoon*, *Jaws.*
Number one on 26 April: 'Bye Bye Baby' by the Bay City Rollers.

The programme for the 1975 final.

Cunningham scores for Glenrothes to win the 1975 final.

Glenrothes, 1974/75 Scottish Cup Junior winners.

Rutherglen Glencairn in 1975.

Above left: The programme for the 1975 semi-final Rugby Park.

Above right: The programme for the 1975 semi-final at Brockville.

APPENDIX 1

THE JUNIOR FOOTBALL HANDBOOK

In 1950 the Glasgow *Evening Citizen* produced The *Junior Football Handbook*, which cost *3d*. This was the first handbook to be devoted exclusively to Junior Football and established an informative directory of all the clubs in Scotland. It consisted of ninety-six pages and was packed with information regarding players, individual club records, league tables, various trophy winners etc. For football enthusiasts it was a joy to read. Despite being well-received, a follow-up wasn't published until 1959, by which time it had doubled in price to *6d*. It was still very informative, but it was sad to see the number of once-famous sides that had folded since the 1950 publication – although some new teams had been formed since then. The following year saw the handbook published for the last time.

Above left: The Evening Citizen Junior Football Handbook 1950/51.

Above middle: The 1959/60 edition.

Above right: The 1960/61 edition.

APPENDIX 2
OTHER PROGRAMMES

Many other programmes involving Junior Football have been produced over the years and the following are a small selection:

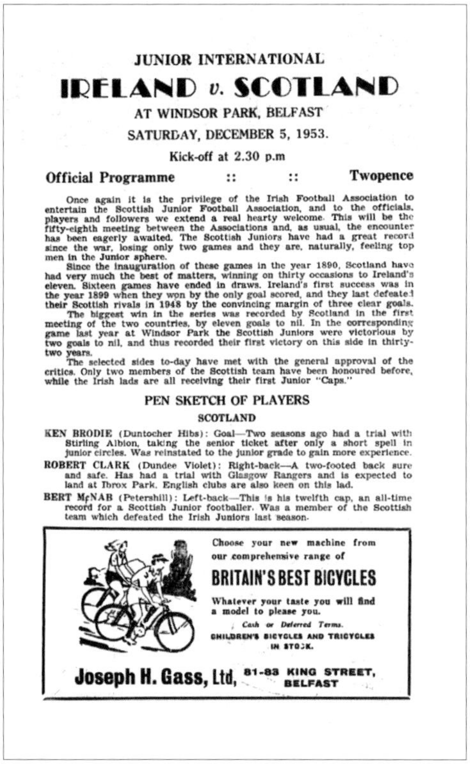

JUNIOR INTERNATIONAL

IRELAND *v.* SCOTLAND

AT WINDSOR PARK, BELFAST

SATURDAY, DECEMBER 5, 1953.

Kick-off at 2.30 p.m

Official Programme :: :: Twopence

Once again it is the privilege of the Irish Football Association to entertain the Scottish Junior Football Association, and to the officials, players and followers we extend a real hearty welcome. This will be the fifty-eighth meeting between the Associations and, as usual, the encounter has been eagerly awaited. The Scottish Juniors have had a great record since the war, losing only two games and they are, naturally, feeling top men in the Junior sphere.

Since the inauguration of these games in the year 1890, Scotland have had very much the best of matters, winning on thirty occasions to Ireland's eleven. Sixteen games have ended in draws. Ireland's first success was in the year 1899 when they won by the only goal scored, and they last defeated their Scottish rivals in 1948 by the convincing margin of three clear goals.

The biggest win in the series was recorded by Scotland in the first meeting of the two countries, by eleven goals to nil. In the corresponding game last year at Windsor Park the Scottish Juniors were victorious by two goals to nil, and thus recorded their first victory on this side in thirty-two years.

The selected sides to-day have met with the general approval of the critics. Only two members of the Scottish team have been honoured before, while the Irish lads are all receiving their first Junior "Caps."

PEN SKETCH OF PLAYERS

SCOTLAND

KEN BRODIE (Duntocher Hibs): Goal—Two seasons ago had a trial with Stirling Albion, taking the senior ticket after only a short spell in junior circles. Was reinstated to the junior grade to gain more experience.

ROBERT CLARK (Dundee Violet): Right-back—A two-footed back sure and safe. Has had a trial with Glasgow Rangers and is expected to land at Ibrox Park. English clubs are also keen on this lad.

BERT McNAB (Petershill): Left-back—This is his twelfth cap, an all-time record for a Scottish Junior footballer. Was a member of the Scottish team which defeated the Irish Juniors last season.

The Football Association of Ireland

cumann peile na héireann

JUNIOR COMMITTEE

Junior International Match

IRELAND

v.

SCOTLAND

DALYMOUNT PARK, DUBLIN

Easter Monday, 6th April, 1953

KICK-OFF :: :: :: 3 P.M.

OFFICE BEARERS AND COMMITTEE, 1952-'53:

Chairman—H. KELLY. **Vice-Chairman**—M. J. McCABE.

Hon. Sec.—K. D. HALPIN **Hon. Treas.**—J. E. GILLIGAN

Secretary—

J. I. WICKHAM, 80 Merrion Square, Dublin

COMMITTEE:

R. Leonard, P. Gray, T. Giffney, G. Goodson, W. Fennell, F. Flanagan, E. Morris, T. Rowan, H. Clarke, P. Gallagher, M. Redmond, W. Thoms, J. J. Horan, D. N. Welch, J. Lydon, J. Feighan, Lieut. F. Byrne, R. J. Doran, C. O'Flynn, V. Deane, J. Younger, C. Liddy, C. Bishop, A. W. Harding.

Official Programme - - - Threepence

PRINTED BY ARDIFF, THE PROGRAMME PRINTER, DUBLIN—D1053

Above left: The programme for a Junior International Ireland *v.* Scotland match held at Windsor Park, Belfast, on 5 December 1953.

Above right: The programme for Junior International Ireland *v.* Scotland match held at Dalymount Park, Dublin, on 6 April 1953. Scotland won 3–0.

SCOTTISH JUNIOR FOOTBALL ASSOCIATION

International

SCOTLAND v. WALES

Easter Road Park — Saturday, 7th March 1953 — Price 3d.

EASTER ROAD PARK has always proved a popular venue for the attractive fare offered by the Scottish Junior Football Association and this afternoon's International game, which is staged by kind permission of the Hibernian Directors, should prove no exception to the general rule.

The Scots team which started the season with such promise, has been given a vote of confidence and they have only to repeat the determination and understanding they showed against the Irishmen, to overcome what will certainly be a dour Welsh opposition today. Reference to previous games since the War, shows that three have been drawn, including the last two, and Scotland's team, a useful blend of youth and mature experience, can be expected to improve on that performance, even though, from a club point of view, the Welshmen seem to enjoy some advantage in familiarity with each others' play.

Four of the Scots players are already trysted to senior sides, but the form of the others is certain to be under close review by the many senior agents who have found these Junior Internationals a happy hunting ground in the past. Quite a few of the men who took part in Scotland's last win over Wales here four years ago, went on to make themselves a senior reputation, including **Robertson,** now Third Lanark's most able goalkeeper.

Scotland's Useful Blend

TEN of the players on view this afternoon are seen in the above picture of the Scottish Junior side which defeated Ireland 5-1 at Firhill Park recently. Stewart (Shettleston) recently went to Dundee and his place is taken by Mackay (Newtongrange Star), whose picture is given below. The players and officials are as follows.—Seated (l. to r.)—Baillie Tom Murray (President, S.J.F.A.), Rae, Divers, Mair, Kelly, Wilson, and Mr J. Kinnear (Secretary, S.J.F.A.). Standing—Mr Frank Smith (Vice-President, S.J.F.A.), Mr Hugh Biggart (Asst. Secretary, S.J.F.A.), Davidson, McNab, Robb, D'Arcy, McBlain, Stewart, and Mr Scoular Lawson (Treasurer, S.J.F.A.). The referee, with his hand on the ball, is Mr T. Bowman, Clydebank.

THIS *Edinburgh Evening News* picture is of **Mackay,** the Newtongrange man who is a provisionally signed Hearts player.

THE WELSH OFFICIALS

HEADING the Welsh party to Edinburgh is Mr R. J. Hughes, president of the North Wales F.A. for nearly half a century—he is in his 83rd year—and a long-service member of the Welsh F.A. Mr Hughes and Mr H. R. Williams, association secretary, are Life Members of the Scottish J.F.A. Of the 27 matches since the first at Bangor in 1911, Mr Hughes has missed only one.

Others in the Welsh contingent include **Mr William Roberts,** of Llandudno, honorary treasurer, one of the best known sporting personalities in Wales, and **Messrs W. F. Morris** (Rhyl) and **R. Gwynfryn Jones** (Llandudno Junction), assistant secretaries. Here, too, is **Mr W. Ewart Williams,** of Llanrwst, treasurer of the influential Welsh League (North), and several members of the League Management Committee.

The Welsh team-manager, **Captain Ralph Tucker**—he was also on duty at Easter Road in 1949 and at Kilmarnock in 1951—is a member of the North Wales F.A. and Welsh League Committees. He played for University College, Bangor, Colwyn Bay, and the famous North of England amateur club, Northern Nomads, and is the present chairman of the combined Bangor Colleges club, "Peritus."

Seeds of friendship between the Scottish J.F.A. (formation year 1886) and the 59-years-old North Wales Coast F.A. were sown at Bangor on April 13, 1912, a union which has become firmly established over the years. That thirteenth day at Bangor certainly turned out to be a lucky one. The North Wales secretary of those days was the late **Lieut.-Col. J. Llewelyn Williams,** Welsh F.A. treasurer. He, too, was a Life Member of the Scottish J.F.A.

Above left: The programme for Junior International Scotland *v.* Wales held at Easter Road on 7 March 1953. Scotland won 3–2. Pictured on the front is Dave MacKay, who at that time was playing for Newtongrange Star. Later he joined Heart of Midlothian.

Above right: The programme for the Irish League 'B' Division *v.* Scottish Central League match held at Grosvenor Park, Belfast on 6 April 1957.

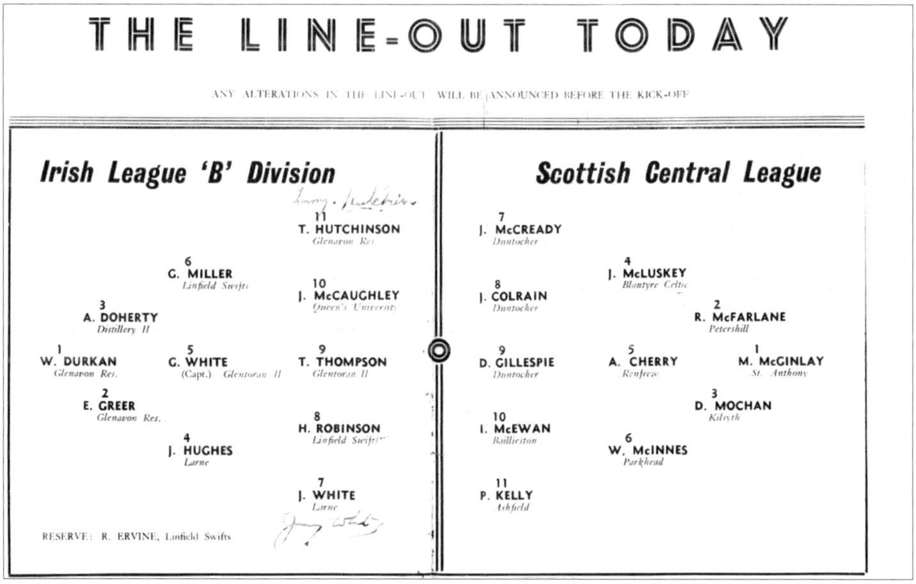

THE LINE-OUT TODAY

ANY ALTERATIONS IN THE LINE-OUT WILL BE ANNOUNCED BEFORE THE KICK-OFF

Irish League 'B' Division

1 W. DURKAN *Glenavon Res.*
2 E. GREER *Glenavon Res.*
3 A. DOHERTY *Distillery II*
4 J. HUGHES *Larne*
5 G. WHITE (Capt.) *Glentoran II*
6 G. MILLER *Linfield Swifts*
7 J. WHITE *Larne*
8 H. ROBINSON *Linfield Swifts*
9 T. THOMPSON *Glentoran II*
10 J. McCAUGHLEY *Queen's University*
11 T. HUTCHINSON *Glenavon Res.*

RESERVE: R. ERVINE, Linfield Swifts

Scottish Central League

1 M. McGINLAY *St. Anthony's*
2 R. McFARLANE *Petershill*
3 D. MOCHAN *Kilsyth*
4 J. McLUSKEY *Blantyre Celtic*
5 A. CHERRY *Renfrew*
6 W. McINNES *Parkhead*
7 J. McCREADY *Duntocher*
8 J. COLRAIN *Duntocher*
9 D. GILLESPIE *Duntocher*
10 I. McEWAN *Baillieston*
11 P. KELLY *Ashfield*

In the Scottish team that day were Denis Mochan of Kilsyth Rangers and John Colrain of Duntocher. Mochan went on to play for Raith Rovers and Dundee United, Colrain for Celtic and Clyde.

Left: A programme for Portsmouth *v.* Scottish Central League *c.* 1937.

Below: The centre pages of the programme.

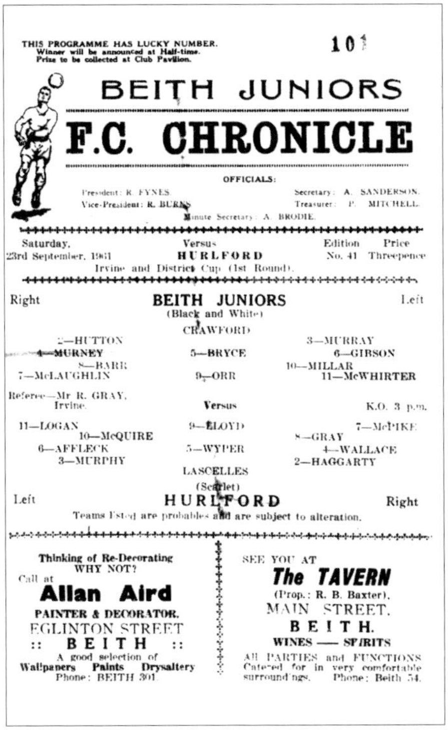

THIS PROGRAMME HAS LUCKY NUMBER.
Winner will be announced at Half-time.
Prize to be collected at Club Pavilion.

101

BEITH JUNIORS

F.C. CHRONICLE

OFFICIALS:

President: R. FYNES. Secretary: A. SANDERSON.
Vice-President: R. BURNS Treasurer: P. MITCHELL.
Minute Secretary: A. BRODIE.

Saturday, 23rd September, 1951 — Versus HURLFORD — Edition No. 41 — Price Threepence
Irvine and District Cup (1st Round).

Right **BEITH JUNIORS** Left
(Black and White)

CRAWFORD
2—HUTTON 3—MURRAY
4—MURNEY 5—BRYCE 6—GIBSON
8—BARR 10—MILLAR
7—McLAUGHLIN 9—ORR 11—McWHIRTER

Referee—Mr R. GRAY, Irvine. **Versus** K.O. 3 p.m.

11—LOGAN 9—LLOYD 7—McPIKE
10—McQUIRE 8—GRAY
6—AFFLECK 5—WYPER 4—WALLACE
3—MURPHY 2—HAGGARTY
LASCELLES
(Scarlet)
Left **HURLFORD** Right

Teams listed are probables and are subject to alteration.

Thinking of Re-Decorating
WHY NOT?
Call at
Allan Aird
PAINTER & DECORATOR.
EGLINTON STREET
:: BEITH ::
A good selection of
Wallpapers Paints Drysaltery
Phone: BEITH 301.

SEE YOU AT
The TAVERN
(Prop.: R. B. Baxter),
MAIN STREET,
BEITH.
WINES —— SPIRITS
All PARTIES and FUNCTIONS Catered for in very comfortable surroundings. Phone: Beith 54.

EAST OF SCOTLAND JUNIOR F.A.
INSTITUTED IN 1896

President WILLIAM WATERSON (Whitburn)
Vice-President JAMES HILL (Rosewell Rosedale)

Secretary PETER CRAIGIE "Edina" The Marches Armadale *Telephone*—Armadale 8

TYNECASTLE PARK 13TH MAY 1950

NEWTONGRANGE STAR v. STONEYBURN JUNIORS

PROGRAMME THREEPENCE

Referee—
W. D. LISTON
Larbert

NEWTONGRANGE STAR
1 McKAY
2 PRYDE
3 ROBERTSON
4 DIXON
5 GORDON
6 PURVES
7 WOOD
8 LINTON
9 KINGHORN
10 ALLAN
11 HOPE

Linesman
J. BISSETT, Edinburgh

STONEYBURN JUNIORS
1 RYAN
2 HENDRY
3 DONNELLY
4 McKEE
5 MICHAEL
6 WILLIAMSON
7 FREW
8 O'CONNELL
9 BOYD
10 FORSYTH
11 JACK

Linesman
A. COOK, Edinburgh

78 and 79 PRINCES STREET, EDINBURGH
THORNTON'S
Telephone CENtral 6576
For All Sports

Above left: A programme issued by Beith Juniors for the first round of the Irvine & District Cup, when they played against Hurlford on 23 September 1951.

Above right: The programme for the Newtongrange Star *v.* Stoneyburn Juniors East of Scotland Cup match played at Tynecastle Park on 13 May 1950.

EAST OF SCOTLAND JUNIOR F.A.
INSTITUTED IN 1896

President WILLIAM WATERSON (Whitburn)
Vice-President JAMES HILL (Rosewell Rosedale)

Secretary PETER CRAIGIE "Edina" The Marches Armadale *Telephone*—Armadale 8

TYNECASTLE PARK 6TH MAY 1950

GLASGOW JUNIOR F.A. v. EAST of SCOTLAND JUNIOR F.A.

PROGRAMME THREEPENCE

Referee—
J. BISSETT
Edinburgh

GLASGOW
1 FORSYTH (Benburb)
2 DOYLE (Maryhill Hearts)
3 CAGGIE (Dennistoun Wav.)
4 BURNETT (Strathclyde)
5 PEARSON (*Capt.*) (Bridgeton Wav.)
6 CREANE (Shawfield)
7 BARTON (Dennistoun Wav.)
8 INNES (Parkhead)
9 BORTHWICK (Shawfield)
10 POLLOCK (Shawfield)
11 DICK (Maryhill)

Linesman
J. FULTON, Edinburgh

EAST of SCOTLAND
1 ROBERTSON (Armadale)
2 McGOWAN (Fauldhouse)
3 GRIFFIN (Rosewell Rosedale)
4 MACKIE (Bathgate Thistle)
5 SKINNER (*Capt.*) (Musselburgh Ath.)
6 GRAHAM (Bonnyrigg Rose A.)
7 BRYSON (Tranent Juniors)
8 CAMPBELL (Loanhead Mayfl'r)
9 GARDENER (Bo'ness United)
10 HAILSTANES (Camelon Juniors)
11 WILLIAMSON (Stoneyburn Jun.)

Linesman
A. COOK, Edinburgh

78 and 79 PRINCES STREET, EDINBURGH
THORNTON'S
Telephone CENtral 6576
For All Sports

Programme for the Glasgow Junior FA *v.* East of Scotland FA match held at Tynecastle Park on 6 May 1950.

APPENDIX 3

SCOTTISH JUNIOR CUP FINAL RESULTS

Year	*Match*	*Score*		
1886/87	Fairfield *v.* Edinburgh Woodburn	3–1[1]		
1887/88	Wishaw Thistle *v.* Maryhill	3–1[1]		
1888/89	Burnbank Swifts *v.* West Benhar Violet	4–1		
1889/90	Burnbank Swifts v. Benburb	3–1[1]		
1890/91	Vale of Clyde *v.* Chryston Athletic	1–1	2–0	
1891/92	Minerva *v.* West Benhar Violet	5–2		
1892/93	Vale of Clyde *v.* Dumbarton Fern	1–1	3–2	
1893/94	Ashfield *v.* Renfrew Victoria	3–0		
1894/95	Ashfield *v.* West Calder Wanderers	1–1	2–1	
1895/96	Cambuslang Hibs *v.* Parkhead	2–1		
1896/97	Strathclyde *v.* Dunfermline Juniors	2–0[1]		
1897/98	Dalziel Rovers *v.* Parkhead	2–1		
1898/99	Parkhead *v.* Westmarch XI	4–1		
1899/1900	Maryhill *v.* Rugby XI	3–2		
1900/01	Burnbank Athletic *v.* Maryhill	2–0		
1901/02	Rutherglen Glencairn *v.* Maryhill	2–2	1–0	
1902/03	Parkhead *v.* Larkhall Thistle	3–0		
1903/04	Vale of Clyde *v.* Parkhead	3–0		
1904/05	Ashfield *v.* Renfrew Victoria	2–1		
1905/06	Dunipace *v.* Kirkintilloch Rob Roy	2–2	1–0	
1906/07	Strathclyde *v.* Maryhill	1–1	1–1	1–0
1907/08	Larkhall Thistle *v.* Queen's Park Hampden XI	1–0		
1908/09	Kilwinning Rangers *v.* Strathclyde	0–0	1–0	
1909/10	Ashfield *v.* Kilwinning Rangers	3–0[1]		
1910/11	Burnbank Athletic *v.* Petershill	1–1	1–0	
1911/12	Petershill *v.* Denny Hibs	5–0		
1912/13	Inverkeithing United *v.* Dunipace	1–0		
1913/14	Larkhall Thistle v. Ashfield	1–1	0–0	1–0
1914/15	Parkhead *v.* Port Glasgow Athletic	2–0		
1915/16	Petershill *v.* Parkhead	2–0		
1916/17	St Mirren Juniors *v.* Renfrew Juniors	0–0	1–0	
1917/18	*Petershill awarded cup – no final played*	—		
1918/19	Rutherglen Glencairn *v.* St. Anthony's	1–1	1–0	

1919/20	Parkhead *v.* Cambuslang Rangers	2–0		
1920/21	Kirkintilloch Rob Roy *v.* Ashfield	1–0		
1921/22	St Roch's *v.* Kilwinning Rangers	2–1[1]		
1922/23	Musselburgh Bruntonians *v.* Arniston Rangers	3–0		
1923/24	Parkhead *v.* Baillieston	1–1	3–1	
1924/25	Saltcoats Victoria *v.* St Anthony's	1–1	3–3	2–1
1925/26	Strathclyde *v.* Bridgeton Waverley	1–1	2–0	
1926/27	Rutherglen Glencairn *v.* Cambuslang Rangers	2–1		
1927/28	Maryhill Hibernians *v.* Burnbank Athletic	6–2		
1928/29	Dundee Violet *v.* Denny Hibs	2–2	4–0[1]	
1929/30	Newtongrange Star *v.* Hall Russell's	3–0		
1930/31	Denny Hibs *v.* Burnbank Athletic	1–0[2]		
1931/32	Glasgow Perthshire *v.* Kirkintilloch Rob Roy	2–1		
1932/33	Yoker Athletic *v.* Tranent Juniors	0–0	4–2	
1933/34	Benburb *v.* Bridgeton Waverley	3–1		
1934/35	Tranent Juniors *v.* Petershill	6–1		
1935/36	Benburb *v.* Yoker Athletic	1–1	1–0	
1936/37	Arthurlie *v.* Kirkintilloch Rob Roy	5–1		
1937/38	Cambuslang Rangers *v.* Benburb	3–2		
1938/39	Rutherglen Glencairn *v.* Shawfield	2–1		
1939/40	Maryhill Juniors *v.* Morton Juniors	1–0		
1940/41	Glasgow Perthshire *v.* Armadale Thistle	2–2	0–0	3–1
1941/42	Clydebank *v.* Vale of Clyde	4–2		
1942/43	Kirkintilloch Rob Roy *v.* Benburb	1–1	0–0	3–1
1943/44	Glasgow Perthshire *v.* Blantyre Victoria	1–0		
1944/45	Burnbank Athletic *v.* Cambuslang Rangers	3–1[1]		
1945/46	Fauldhouse United *v.* Arthurlie	2–0		
1946/47	Shawfield *v.* Bo'ness United	1–1	2–1	
1947/48	Bo'ness United *v.* Irvine Meadow XI	2–1		
1948/49	Auchinleck Talbot *v.* Petershill	3–2		
1949/50	Blantyre Victoria *v.* Cumnock Juniors	3–0		
1950/51	Petershill *v.* Irvine Meadow XI	1–0		
1951/52	Kilbirnie Ladeside *v.* Camelon Juniors	1–0		
1952/53	Vale of Leven *v.* Annbank United	1–0		
1953/54	Sunnybank *v.* Lochee Harp	2–1		
1954/55	Kilsyth Rangers *v.* Duntocher Hibs	0–0	4–1	
1955/56	Petershill *v.* Lugar Boswell Thistle	4–1		
1956/57	Banks o' Dee *v.* Kilsyth Rangers	1–0		
1957/58	Shotts Bon Accord *v.* Pumpherston	2–0		
1958/59	Irvine Meadow XI *v.* Shettleston	2–1		
1959/60	St Andrews United *v.* Greenock Juniors	3–1		
1960/61	Dunbar United *v.* Cambuslang Rangers	2–2	2–0	
1961/62	Kirkintilloch Rob Roy *v.* Renfrew Juniors	1–1	1–0	
1962/63	Irvine Meadow XI *v.* Glenafton Athletic	2–1		
1963/64	Johnstone Burgh *v.* Cambuslang Rangers	1–1	3–0	

1964/65	Linlithgow Rose *v.* Baillieston Juniors	4–1		
1965/66	Bonnyrigg Rose Athletic *v.* Whitburn	1–1	6–1	
1966/67	Kilsyth Rangers *v.* Rutherglen Glencairn	1–1	3–1	
1967/68	Johnstone Burgh *v.* Glenrothes	2–2	4–3	
1968/69	Cambuslang Rangers v. Kirkintilloch Rob Roy	1–0		
1969/70	Blantyre Victoria *v.* Penicuik	1–1	1–0	
1970/71	Cambuslang Rangers *v.* Newtongrange Star	2–1		
1971/72	Cambuslang Rangers *v.* Bonnyrigg Rose Ath.	1–1	3–2	
1972/73	Irvine Meadow XI *v.* Cambuslang Rangers	2–2	3–3	1–0
1973/74	Cambuslang Rangers *v.* Linlithgow Rose	3–1		
1974/75	Glenrothes *v.* Rutherglen Glencairn	1–0		
1975/76	Bo'ness United *v.* Darvel Juniors	3–0		
1976/77	Kilbirnie Ladeside *v.* Kirkintilloch Rob Roy	3–1		
1977/78	Bonnyrigg Rose Athletic *v.* Stonehouse Violet	1–0		
1978/79	Cumnock Juniors *v.* Bo'ness United	1–0		
1979/80	Baillieston *v.* Benburb	2–2	2–0	
1980/81	Pollock *v.* Arthurlie	1–0		
1981/82	Blantyre Victoria *v.* Baillieston	1–0		
1982/83	East Kilbride Thistle *v.* Bo'ness United	2–0		
1983/84	Bo'ness United *v.* Baillieston	2–0		
1984/85	Pollock *v.* Petershill	3–1		
1985/86	Auchinleck Talbot *v.* Pollock	3–2		
1986/87	Auchinleck Talbot *v.* Kilbirnie Ladeside	1–1	1–0	
1987/88	Auchinleck Talbot *v.* Petershill	1–0		
1988/89	Cumnock Juniors *v.* Ormiston Primrose	1–0		
1989/90	Hill o' Beath *v.* Lesmahagow	1–0		
1990/91	Auchinleck Talbot *v.* Newtongrange Star	1–0		
1991/92	Auchinleck Talbot *v.* Glenafton Athletic	4–0		
1992/93	Glenafton Athletic *v.* Tayport	1–0		
1993/94	Largs Thistle *v.* Glenafton Athletic	1–0		
1994/95	Camelon Juniors *v.* Whitburn	2–0		
1995/96	Tayport *v.* Camelon	2–0[3]		
1996/97	Pollock *v.* Tayport	3–1		
1997/98	Arthurlie *v.* Pollock	4–0		
1998/99	Kilwinning Rangers *v.* Kelty Hearts	1–0		
1999/2000	Whitburn *v.* Johnstone Burgh	2–2[3]	4–3[4]	
2000/01	Renfrew *v.* Carnoustie Panmure	0–0[3]	6–5[4]	
2001/02	Linlithgow Rose *v.* Auchinleck Talbot	1–0		
2002/03	Tayport *v.* Linlithgow Rose	1–0[3]		
2003/04	Carnoustie Panmure *v.* Tayport	0–0[3]	4–1[4]	
2004/05	Tayport *v.* Lochee United	2–0		
2005/06	Auchinleck Talbot *v.* Bathgate Thistle	2–1		
2006/07	Linlithgow Rose *v.* Kelty Hearts	2–1[3]		
2007/08	Bathgate Thistle *v.* Cumnock	2–1		
2008/09	Auchinleck Talbot *v.* Clydebank	2–1		

2009/10	Linlithgow Rose *v.* Largs Thistle	1–0
2010/11	Auchinleck Talbot *v.* Musselburgh	2–1[3]

[1]After protest
[2]Protested but not replayed
[3]After extra time
[4]Penalties